BRADSHAW'S GUIDE

WEST COAST MAIN LINE MANCHESTER TO GLASGOW

John Christopher &
Campbell McCutcheon

AMBERLEY

Punch's Rough Railway Guide
First Tourist. 'Where for, ma'am?"

Old Lady. 'There! Lawk a mercy if
I haven't forgot. Oh! mister, please
run over a few of the willages on this
railway, will yer?'

About this book
Bradshaw's Guide explores many aspects of the railway journeys to be had on Scotland's railways. Through Bradshaw's text and the supportive images, the lines are described, and main features shown. Of course, some of the lines have been closed and others have opened since Bradshaw compiled this guide in 1863. Hopefully, it will encourage you to delve into the history of the railways of the West Coast Main Line and encourage you to visit some otherwise bypassed town. Please note that public access to railway lines is restricted for reasons of safety.

First published 2014

Amberley Publishing
The Hill, Stroud
Gloucestershire, GL5 4EP

www.amberley-books.com

Copyright © Campbell McCutcheon and
John Christopher, 2014

The right of Campbell McCutcheon and John
Christopher to be identified as the Authors of this
work has been asserted in accordance with the
Copyrights, Designs and Patents Act 1988.

ISBN 978 1 4456 4041 9 (print)
ISBN 978 1 4456 4074 7 (ebook)

British Library Cataloguing in Publication Data.
A catalogue record for this book is available from
the British Library.

Typeset in 9.5pt on 12pt Celeste.
Typesetting by Amberley Publishing.
Printed in the UK.

Bradshaw on the WCML

A haggis is a pudding exclusively Scotch, but considered of French origin. Its ingredients are oatmeal, suet, pepper, &c., and it is usually boiled in a sheep's stomach. Although a heavy, yet it is by no means a disagreeable dish.

Bradshaw's Guide, as it is commonly known thanks to a certain TV programme, covers the length and breadth of Britain, along the existing railway routes of the 1860s. Britain's major routes had, by then, been built but there were still many places that were without a railway. Interestingly, too, many of the sights of the Victorian and Edwardian era we take for granted nowadays had yet to be built. There was no Blackpool Tower, Liverpool's dock system had not grown to the extent it reached in the early twentieth century, Manchester was without a ship canal directly connecting it with the sea and Glasgow was without the world-renowned architecture of Charles Rennie MacIntosh.

Bradshaw's Descriptive Railway Hand-Book of Great Britain and Ireland is more than a tome describing the railway routes in existence in 1863 and is a genuinely informative guidebook of the most important places in Britain. This book is one of a series published by Amberley which helps bring Bradshaw into the twenty-first century, giving the reader a font that is readable and a breadth of illustrative material that helps to portray the West Coast Main Line that the Bradshaw's Guide writers would have seen on their travels in 1861–63 as they compiled the guide. Three parts will bring the Premier Route of the 1860s to life, with this, the second, primarily concerning itself with the area from Macclesfield and Warrington to Glasgow and Edinburgh. Ultimately, the series, which already covers the lines of Isambard Kingdom Brunel, the Great Western Railway and the South East of England, will encompass all of the railways of the United Kingdom and of Ireland.

Bradshaw and The West Coast Main Line

George Bradshaw was born in 1801 and died in 1853 at the age of fifty-two. His publishing empire had begun in the canal age, and he produced a series of maps and guides of Britain's canals. With the advent of the railways, his attention turned to guides to the new form of transport and, by 1863, his guide covered the whole of the United Kingdom. The West Coast Main Line (WCML) as a concept did not exist at the time. The railways going north from London had been built in a haphazard way, each company responsible for but a section. Eventually, by the 1850s, the main route to Scotland was operated by just two companies – the London & North Western (LNWR) and the Caledonian (or Caley, as it was affectionaly known). Parts of the route now operated as part of the WCML were operated by the Lancashire & Yorkshire Railway and the route itself deviates at Cheadle Hulme and Crewe to form two distinct lines travelling north, one going via Warrington Bank Quay and the other via Manchester and Bolton. The route crosses the Liverpool & Manchester Railway, one of Britain's oldest, and we travel the important route between Liverpool and its inland neighbour on the way to Scotland, where the line splits at Carstairs, taking the intrepid passenger to Edinburgh or Glasgow.

It is fair to say that the railways are the Victorians' greatest legacy to the twentieth and twenty-first centuries. They shrank space and time. Before their coming different parts of the country had existed in local time based on the position of the sun, with Bristol, for example, running ten minutes behind London. The Great Western Railway changed all that in 1840 when it applied synchronised railway time throughout its area. The presence of the railways defined the shape and development of many of our towns and cities, they altered the distribution of the population and forever changed the fundamental patterns of our lives. For many millions of Britons the daily business of where they live and work, and how they travel between the two, is defined by the network of iron rails laid down nearly two centuries ago by the engineers and an anonymous army of railway navvies.

The timing of the publication of Bradshaw's guidebooks is interesting. This particular account is taken from the 1863 edition of the handbook although, for practical reasons, it must have been written slightly earlier, probably between 1860 and 1862. By this stage the railways had lost their pioneering status, and with the heady days of the railway mania of the 1840s over they were settling into the daily business of transporting people and goods. By the early 1860s the main line from Glasgow to London, for example, had been in operation for around twenty years. It was also by this time that rail travel had become sufficiently commonplace to create a market for Bradshaw's guides.

As a young man George Bradshaw had been apprenticed to an engraver in Manchester in 1820, and after a spell in Belfast he returned to Manchester to set up his own business as an engraver and printer specialising principally in maps. In October 1839 he produced the world's first compilation of railway timetables. Entitled *Bradshaw's Railway Time Tables and Assistant to Railway Travelling*, the slender cloth-bound volume sold for sixpence. By 1840 the title had changed to *Bradshaw's Railway Companion* and the price doubled to one shilling. It then evolved into a monthly publication with the price reduced to the original and more affordable sixpence.

Although George Bradshaw died in 1853 the company continued to produce the monthly guides and in 1863 it launched Bradshaw's *Descriptive Railway Hand-Book of Great Britain and Ireland* (which forms the basis of this series of books). It was originally published in four sections as proper guidebooks without any of the timetable information of the monthly publications. Universally referred to as Bradshaw's Guide it is this guidebook that features in Michael Portillo's *Great British Railway Journeys*, and as a result of its exposure to a new audience the book found itself catapulted into the bestseller list over 150 years after it was originally published.

Without a doubt the Bradshaw Guides were invaluable in their time and they provide the modern-day reader with a fascinating insight into the mid-Victorian rail traveller's experience. In 1865 *Punch* had praised Bradshaw's publications, stating that 'seldom has the gigantic intellect of man been employed upon a work of greater utility'. Having said that, the usual facsimile editions available nowadays don't make especially easy reading with their columns of close-set type. There are scarcely any illustrations for a start, and attempts to trace linear journeys from A to B are interrupted by distracting branch line diversions. That's where this volume comes into its own. *Bradshaw's Guide to the West Coast Main Line* takes the reader on a continuous journey from the the top end of Cheshire all the way to the Second City of the Empire and also to Scotland's capital city. The illustrations show scenes from Victorian and Edwardian times and they are juxtaposed with photographs of the locations in more recent times. The accompanying information provides greater background detail on the sights to be seen, the railways and the many locations along the route.

The railways

In 1863, the West Coast Main Line was a 399-mile route from London to Glasgow., travelling from Euston via Watford, Milton Keynes, Rugby, Nuneaton, Stafford, Crewe, Warrington, Wigan, Preston, Lancaster, Oxenholme, Penrith, Carlisle and Motherwell to Glasgow Bridge Street. Numerous branches now serve some of Britain's largest cities, including Birmingham, Coventry, Manchester and Liverpool.

Due to the nature of the line, it is very twisty, following natural contours. It lacked many of the advantages of the East Coast Main Line and numerous efforts have been made to create trains that tilt to help speed the flow of trains. The 1970s APT was a failure but the Pendolino of today is a resounding

Left: George Bradshaw, the man behind the famous guides.

Left: An advertising poster for the streamlined expresses on the East and West Coast main lines.

Above: Another poster, this time for the Advanced Passenger Train, APT, the 1970s–80s tilting train, which was cancelled in the early 1980s.

THE FIRST "BRADSHAW"
A reminiscence of Whitsun Holidays in Ancient Egypt.   From an old-time tabl(e)ature

Above: Punch pokes some gentle fun at the ubiquitous nature of the Bradshaw publications, which included timetables and guides or 'hand-books'. Although George Bradshaw had died in 1853, the publications continued to be known by his name.

success. Trains of the 1850s took over twelve hours to reach each terminus but nowadays, the journey time is around four hours thirty minutes.

Originally built as a series of separate companies, by 1863, the Premier Route was owned by two separate companies, with England being covered by the London & North Westrn Railway and Scotland by the Caledonian. From early on, the rolling stock used was West Coast Joint Stock, part owned by each company. In 1923, for the first time, with the amalgamation of the various railways in Britain into four large companies, the route was managed by one company. By the late 1920s, the Royal Scot locomotives had been introduced, reducing the journey time and having a non-stop run from Euston to Carlisle, at the time the longest in the world. By 1937, with the Coronation Scot streamlined locomotives, the non-stop run took you all the way and in 1937 an LMS locomotive on the WCML captured briefly the world record for steam locomotives, 114 mph. The main route was electrified totally by 1974, paving the way for new locomotives and a new coaches design, the Mk3. When the railways were privatised and Virgin won the WCML franchise, the new Pendolinos were introduced. A sleeper service was introduced in the late Victorian era and Caledonian sleepers still operate today. Investment in the WCML continues with quadrupling of track and planned electrifications of branches. Bradshaw may recognise the route but not the speed and quality of service. Enjoy this journey on the railways of 1863.

PICKING UP MAIL BAGS AT FULL SPEED

Above: On Bradshaw's railway, one of the most important forms of traffic was the mail train. On this LNWR official postcard, issued by the company around 1903, we see how mail bags were collected by a moving train.

Left: Benja Fold, Bramhall, typical of much of the architecture of this part of Cheshire. These cottages are of box construction, timber framed, and date from the sixteenth century. At Cheadle Junction is the union between WCML and the route to Manchester and Bolton.

Cheshire and Lancashire

LANCASHIRE

A maritime county, situated on the north-western coast of England. This county includes part of the great coal fields of the north of England, and this circumstance, combined with its natural advantages for trade and manufactures, has gradually raised it to the rank of the greatest manufacturing county in the kingdom, containing Manchester, the centre of cotton manufacture, and Liverpool, the great emporium of commerce for that side of our island. The soil and surface of the county are various; and its features in some parts, particularly towards the north, and all along its eastern border, are strongly marked. Here the hills are in general bold and lofty and the valleys narrow and picturesque. On the seacoast, and nearly the whole of the southern side of the county, following the course of the River Mersey, the land is low and flat. Moorlands are much more extensive than might have been expected in so populous a district, and where land is consequently very valuable. The manufactures of Lancashire are the most extensive in the kingdom, chiefly those of cotton, in all its branches; also of silk, woollen, linen, hats, stockings, pins, needles, nails, watch tools and movements (nearly the whole of which that are used in the United Kingdom being made in this county), tobacco, snuff, glass, earthenware, porcelain, paper, etc.

The cotton trade, of which Lancashire engrosses by far the greatest share, has risen to an extent, and with rapidity beyond example. Manchester is the principal seat of this vast manufacture. From thence it spreads on all sides, to the south and east into Cheshire and Yorkshire, over the greater part of Lancashire, extending from Furness to Derby on the one hand, and from Liverpool to Halifax on the other. The raw material being principally collected in Liverpool, it is thence distributed to all parts of the surrounding districts, where thousands are employed in preparing it, from that depot to be sent to all parts of the world. Around Manchester, various of the principal towns and villages form subordinate stations of this extensive traffic, each being the centre of its own little sphere. Of these secondary towns, the principal are Bolton, Blackburn, Wigan, and Preston, on the west and north; Stockport on the south, and Ashton on the east. A variety of other employments, as those of bleachers, dyers, printers, tool-makers, engine and machine makers, etc. entirely depend for their existence on this manufacture. The commerce of Lancashire consists principally in the exchange of its manufactured goods; Liverpool engrosses nearly the whole of the export trade, and has risen accordingly, within less than two centuries, from a small village to its present importance.

Left: Cotton is what made Lancashire such an industrious county. It had just the right climate for cotton manufacture, with damp, cool conditions, but also inventors such as Samuel Crompton, of Bolton, who revolutionised the cotton industry with the invention of the spinny mule. This view shows the house where he was born in Bolton.

Below: An advert postcard for Richard Haworth, Tatton Mills, Ordsall, Manchester. These machines are washing the cotton before it is woven. The noise here would have been bearable but in the spinning mills, the clack of machinery was deafening with hundreds of looms side by side.

LONDON AND NORTH WESTERN

Macclesfield to Cheadle Junction

PRESTBURY

Population, 358.
Telegraph station at Macclesfield, 2¼ miles.
Money Order Office at Macclesfield, 2¼ miles.

Here is a curious old church, which has recently undergone considerable improvements and decorations. The curious old Norman chapel, distinct from the church, is appropriated as a National and Sunday school. In 1808, tumuli, urns, and human bones were found here. In the vicinity are Adlington Hall, seat of C. Legh, Esq., which was besieged for a fortnight by the parliamentarians; Bulky Hall; W. Brocklehurst, Esq., Mottram Park; Rev. H. Wright, Styperson Park; Shrigley Hall, Rev. B. Lowther.

Passing Adlington station, we arrive at

POYNTON

Population, 1,284.
Telegraph station at Stockport, 5½ miles.
Money Order Office at Stockport, 5½ miles.

In the vicinity is Poynton Hall, seat of Lord Vernon, who rebuilt it, together with St Mary's Church, in 1789; and about 11 miles to the east, Lyme Hall, T. Legh, Esq., is partly ancient, and stands in a vast park, or forest, once abounding in red deer. Sir Perkin a Legh was the favourite follower of the Black Prince, from whom the estate was inherited; their pictures are preserved here (in armour), with the Prince's bed, and other relics. It is a question, however, if the portraits are authentic, though they are undoubtedly ancient.

BRAMHALL

Population, 1,615. Distance from station, ½ mile.
Telegraph station at Stockport, 4 miles.

Close at hand is Bramhall House, a fine timber residence of the 16th century, partly modernised. It contains portraits of Sir A. Legh, of Adlington, who was at one time said to be Percy's hero, 'Will you hear a Spanish lady,' in his Reliques, but which applied to Sir J. Belle, of Thorpe, who was present at the siege of Cadiz.

Cheadle Junction, point of union with the mainline from Crewe to Manchester.

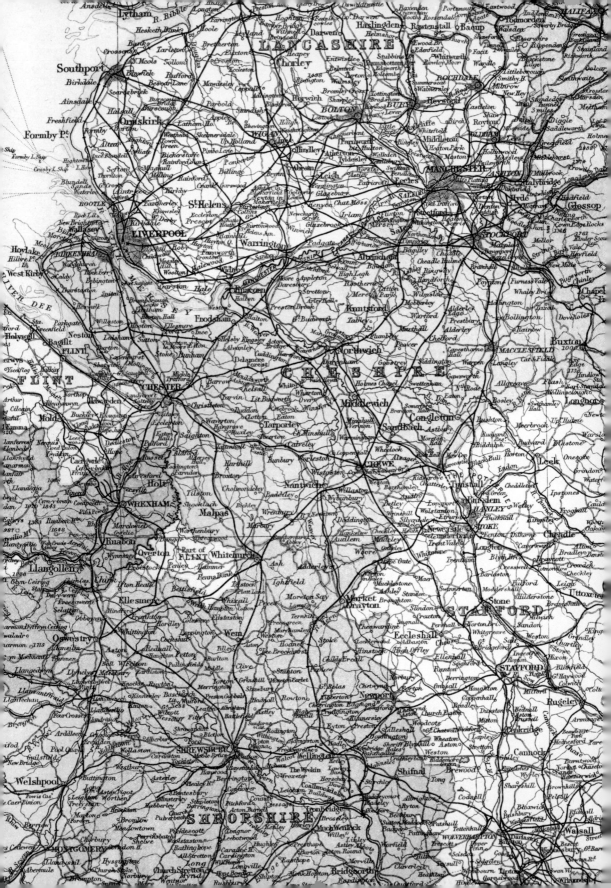

Norton Park, seat of Sir R. Brooke, Bart. The basement story of the priory still contains some most interesting Norman remains, in a state of good preservation.

The line then proceeds through the Moore Hill excavations, and reaches

MOORE

Population, 269.
Telegraph station at Warrington, 3 miles.
Money Order Office at Warrington, 3 miles.

The pretty village of this name is situated to the eastward of the line, but is not in view.

Soon after leaving this station we reach the Arpley embankment, and pass over the Mersey Viaduct. This, though less grand in appearance than the Dutton Viaduct, is a fine work, consisting of twelve arches, through three of which the River Mersey and the Mersey and Irwell canal pass. The valley of the Mersey is spread before us, and on each side the scenery is very beautiful, consisting principally of rich pasture land, adorned with farmhouses and cottages.

A short distance beyond this the river winds towards the town of Warrington, with its manufactory chimneys, large buildings, and churches, etc. Continuing along the embankment the train soon arrives at

WARRINGTON

A telegraph station. Hotels: Lion, Nag's Head.
Market Days: Wednesdays and Saturdays.
Fairs: Every other Wednesday, July 18th and November 30th; on alternate Wednesdays for cattle.
Bankers: Parr, Lyon and Co.; Branch of Manchester and Liverpool District Banking Company.

Warrington is an interesting old town on the River Mersey, in Lancashire, 181 miles from London, and about 21 miles from Manchester and Liverpool. The river is free from the sea to this point, above which it belongs to the Mersey and Irwell Navigation Company, represented by the late Earl of Ellesmere. Vessels of 150 tons can get up to Bank Quay in the spring tides.

This town in the oldest documents (temp. Henry III) is called Werinton. It is on the line of the great Roman road from south to north, and considerable remains of this early period have been found at Wilderspool and Stockton Heath, on the left bank of the Mersey, which is supposed to have been the emulate of the Itineraries. Here the Royalist army, under General Bailey, after having been defeated at Preston, by Cromwell, in 1648, surrendered prisoners of war. In 1745, the central arches of the bridge (built by the Earl of Derby in the reign of Henry VII) were broken down, to impede the march of Prince Charles and the Scotch army.

Population, 26,947. One member is returned to parliament. Cotton and

Left: The royal visit to Crosfield's Works, Warrington. These were located close to Warrington Bank Quay railway station and produced soaps, alkalis and other chemicals. They were bought by Unilever and sold to Ineos in 2001.

Middle and left: Two inspection trains on the LNWR. The above photo shows the locomotive *Carlisle* complete with carriage. Below was F. W. Webb's personal inspection train, hauled by *Locomotion.* He was the locomotive engineer of the LNWR from 1871–1903.

fustian goods, pins, glass, and tools of various kinds, are manufactured here. It has an old-fashioned look, with several narrow streets, and contained many timbered picturesque houses most of which, however, are pulled down and have given place to ornamented windows and plate glass; one good specimen still remains in the Market Place. The Sessions House and Bridewell were built under an Improvement Act in the year 1840. The church is a large building; the chancel and the arches supporting the tower are good; decorated with a crypt at the east end. The Butler Chapel is late perpendicular, and contains a very fine altar tomb of the 15th century; the tower is of the end of the 17th century, the rest of the building is modern. The Butlers, who held this and various other manors from the time of Henry III, became extinct in the reign of Elizabeth; the manor is now the property of J. Ireland Blackburne, Esq., of Hale, and the advowson of the Rectory belongs to Lord Lilford. The Free School was founded under the will of Sir Thomas Boteler in 1526. The Mote Hill, probably the original seat of the Lords of Warrington, is now covered with the Diocesan and Orphan Schools.

There was an academy founded here in the last century, described by Mrs Barbauld as 'the nursery of men for future years'. Priestly, Enfield, Gilbert Wakefield, Taylor, and Aikin, the father of Mrs Barbauld, were amongst the professors, and many of their works were printed at Eyres' press in the town. A good substantial building has been erected in Bold Street, containing a Public Museum and Library, and rooms occupied as a School of Art. It has been built by public subscription, and is the property of the corporation.

In the neighbourhood are; Frinteick Hall, the seat of Rev. F. Hopwood, and a church, in which are effigies, etc., of the Leghs of Lyme, whose ancestor is said to have won his lands in the battle of Agincourt. Sankey gives name to the Sankey Canal, which, beginning at St Helens, bends round to Warrington, and comes out opposite Runcorn, a circuit of 15½ miles, 12 of which were cut between 1755 and 1758, when no other canal existed in England, so that this deserves notice as being the eldest of the kind. A direct railway now runs from St Helens to its outlet. Bold Hall is the seat of Sir H. Bold Hoghton, who represents the old family of Bold, its former residents for many generations. They give name to Bold Street, in Liverpool. On the Cheshire side of the Mersey a low range of hills of new red sandstone extends from Runcorn to Dunham, affording many rich and beautiful prospects. Halton Castle is a picturesque ruin on one of the higher portions of this range. The famous Bridgewater Canal passes this way (near some later cuttings for improving the Mersey navigation). It was cut on a level by Brindley for the Duke of Bridgewater, being 38 miles long from Manchester, through Worsley and Altrincham, and crosses the Bollin by an aqueduct half-a-mile long. The Duke expended all his capital in the construction, but lived to realise a vast fortune by his perseverance. His first efforts were to reduce the carriage of goods and price of coals 50 per cent. It is said that when the Manchester and Liverpool Railway was projected the Bridgewater agent was asked to take shares in the concern; but he had, it seems, such confidence in the

Above: Wigan Junction Colliery. Wigan produced an excellent cannel coal, much prized and sought after. Women were employed until the twentieth century above ground as pit brow lassies.

Middle left: Wigan Pier in 1966. Wigan's pier was made famous by George Orwell in his book *The Road to Wigan Pier*. As a treatise on life during the Depression in industrial England, there is no finer descriptive text.

Bottom left: Wigan was famous for its cotton mills but the mining industry in the town was catered for by specialist companies. This view shows a fan for ventilation made by Walker Brothers.

superiority of the old canal over the new plan of communication, that he would consent only to take 'all or none.'

Warrington Junction, Newton Bridge, and Preston Junction stations.

Preston and Parkside.

Preston Junction to Preston

GOLBORNE
Golborne Park, seat of J. Catterall, Esq.

WIGAN
A telegraph station.
Hotels: Clarence; Victoria; Royal.
Market Days: Mondays and Fridays.
Fairs: Holy Thursday, June 27th, Oct. 28th.
Bankers: Manchester and Liverpool District Banking Co.; Woodcock & Sons.

A great cotton town in Lancashire, and a parliamentary borough (two members), near the head of the River Douglas. Population, 37,658. Contains stone and coal in great abundance. The town is well built on the whole, but straggling. Some parts are ancient; the newest houses are on the east side. The large church of All Saints, with its tower, is older than Edward III's time. The greater portion of it was rebuilt about 1853. It contains monuments of the Bradshaighs and other lords of the manor. It is a rectory, the value of which exceeds £4,000 a-year, the rector being lord of the manor. The Town Hall, near it, was rebuilt in 1720. There are about twenty large factories, employing about 10,000 hands. Bishop Woolton and Dr Leyland were natives.

Much cannel coal is found near Wigan. It is a beautiful jetty black which takes a polish, and is capable of being worked into blocks for building, as well as for ornaments. In digging for coal, some years back, a sulphur spring was discovered near Scholes Bridge, over which a pump-room, etc., were built, and the place styled New Harrogate, but it is now disused.

Wigan, a little while ago, could boast of having the tallest chimney in England. It was exactly 400 ft. high, and took four years to build, being designed for the chemical works; but it fell down. Another, only 3 ft. lower, built for Muspratt's works at Newton, was blown down with gunpowder in 1853. There is a Grammar School in Millgate. In Wigan Lane, the northern outlet of the town, there stands a pillar to the memory of Sir T. Tyldesley, who fell in the battle of 25th August, 1651, when the Earl of Derby with 600 horse was defeated by Col. Lilburne. The Earl was beheaded at Bolton six weeks afterwards. He

Left: Church Street, Preston, *c.* 1903. Dick, Kerr manufactured trams in Preston.

Below: HMS *Gleaner* in Preston's docks in May 1951. Thomas W. Ward, a Sheffield industrial combine and steel mill owner, broke ships at Preston.

MODEL OF PROPOSED PRESTON POWER STATION.

Left: With around fifty cotton mills in the town, Preston was always a large industrial centre. As well as the mills, cars (the Bond Minicar and Bug) and aircraft have been made here too. This view shows a model of the new Preston power station at the 1922 Preston Guild.

had sustained two defeats in this town in 1643, so that Wigan was unfortunate. Cromwell's Ditch, a cut of the Douglas, on the township border, commemorates a visit paid by him when in pursuit of the Duke of Hamilton in 1648.

Part of a Roman road may be traced towards Standish; it is straight as an arrow for 1½ mile.

STANDISH
    Population, 3,054.
    Distance from station, ¼ mile.
    Telegraph station at Wigan, 2¼ miles.
    Hotels: Eagle and Child.
    Fairs: June 29th and Nov. 22nd.
    Money Order Office at Wigan, 2¼ miles.

Standish is the seat of the Standishes, a very ancient family. Haigh Hall, the seat of the Bari of Crawford and Balcarres, a descendant of the Bradshaighs, who lived here for many centuries. Ashton Hall, a fine seat, is in the district of Mackerfield.

COPPULL
    Telegraph station at Buxton, 3¾ miles.

This place derives its name from a copse close to it. Near is Chisnall Hall, which was the old seat of the Chisnalls; to the left is Wrightington Hall, an old mansion.

Euxton: Euxton Hall, the seat of W. M. J. Anderton, Esq.

LEYLAND
    Population, 3,755.
    Telegraph station at Euxton, 1½ mile.
    Hotel: Railway.
    Money Order Office at Chorley, 4 miles.

Here is an excellent Free Grammar School, and old church, with the tombs of the Farringtons, of Worden Hall.

FARINGTON.
    Population, 1,791.
    A telegraph station.

Cuerden Hall, the seat of R. Townley Parker, Esq.

PHAROS LIGHTHOUSE
FLEETWOOD

Above: A Coronation Scot locomotive in the snow north of Preston in 1937. Introduced in 1937, the Coronation Scots were streamlined and painted in Caledonian blue, with white stripes. Their carriages were also streamlined. A Coronation Scot briefly held the world speed record for a railway locomotive in 1937, achieving 114 mph close to Crewe.

Left: Close to Preston is the fishing town of Fleetwood. This view shows the Pharos lighthouse being used as a signboard, complete with directions to the railway station.

PRESTON

A telegraph station.

Hotels: Ball; Victoria; Red Lion; Castle.

Market Days: Wednesday, Friday, and Saturday.

Fairs: Week before first Sunday after Epiphany, March 27th, August 25th, and November 7th.

Bankers: Roskell & Co.; Branch Lancaster Banking Co.; Preston Banking Co.

An ancient borough (two members) and an important cotton manufacturing town in Lancashire, population 82,985, standing some distance without the manufacturing circle, on a bill above the beautiful valley of the Ribble, 210 miles from London. Below the town the river widens considerably. Recent improvements in its navigation have enabled vessels of large tonnage to reach the town. Preston is a place of some historic importance. King John and two of the Edwards, John O'Gaunt, and James the First, visited the town. Cromwell defeated the royalist forces in the suburbs. The first Scottish rebellion in 1715 was quelled here, and the young Pretender passed through in 1745. Henry the First granted it a charter, and successive sovereigns have confirmed and extended its municipal privileges. One of its most peculiar institutions is its ancient guild, held every twenty years, at which the aristocracy of the county have been wont to assemble as participants in the festivities which distinguish it. In past times Preston was noted for the gentility of its inhabitants. Many Lancashire families made it their occasional residence, and it was, before the introduction of the cotton trade, according to Dr Whitaker (*History of Richmondshire*), 'an elegant and economical town, the resort of well-born but ill-portioned and ill-endowed old maids and widows.' In 1771 the first cotton mill was erected, and since that time the staple trade of Lancashire has so extended within it that Preston has become one of the principal manufacturing towns in the county. There are upwards of fifty cotton mills in the town, the largest establishment being that of Messrs Horrockses, Miller, and Co., who employ upwards of 3,000 hands. The commercial annals of this town are memorable from two long continued disputes between the employers and employed. The strike or lock-out of 1836–37 lasted fourteen weeks, and caused vast distress in the town; that of 1853–54 was prolonged to a period of thirty-nine weeks, during which 15,000 or 16,000 persons were out of employment, and the greater portion of the factories were entirely closed. The order which was preserved in the town, the good conduct of the operatives, and the support which they received from their class in other towns, were much noticed at the time.

Preston is a well-built town, with some old streets and houses. Its parish church has been recently rebuilt, and all the other churches are modern. The town hall is a structure quite unworthy the town, which is singularly deficient in handsome public buildings, for, excepting the elegant edifice erected as the Mechanics' Institution, and the pile comprising the Grammar

Above and middle left: In competition with the East Coast Main Line's Flying Scotsman, the LMS introduced the Royal Scot, with the world's longest non-stop run. From Euston to Carlisle was 299¼ miles and the Royal Scot class of locomotives took the train north to Edinburgh and Glasgow, leaving at 10 a.m. The *Royal Scot* locomotive, No. 6100, even managed to travel around the USA and Canada on a promotional tour. Without assistance, she climbed 5,600 feet into the Rockies.

GROVE STREET, WILMSLOW

Left: Grove Street, Wilmslow, in the 1950s.

School, the Literary and Philosophical Institution, and the Winckley Club, it scarcely possesses any building of architectural importance.

Although Preston was so aristocratic a town in days of yore, it possessed before the passing of the Reform Act, the only real democratic electoral suffrage in the kingdom; all its inhabitants of six months' residence, and above twenty-one years of age, if free from the taint of pauperism, were entitled to a vote. The Stanleys were long the patrons of the borough, but the democratic suffrage had occasionally democratic suitors. Cobbett was once a candidate for its representation, and Henry Hunt sat in two parliaments for Preston.

Preston is unrivalled for the beauty of its situation, and few towns are so well off for public walks, and these are to be yet further extended. Sir Richard Arkwright, the great improver of the first spinning frame, was a native of Preston; Lady Hamilton, the friend of Nelson, is also said to have been born here.

In the neighbourhood of Preston are Tulheth Hall, the seat of the monastic community who afterwards settled at Furness Abbey; Penwortham Priory, erected on the site of the ancient priory, that was a cell of the Abbey of Evesham; the Castle Hill; Penwortham, the site of a castle mentioned in Domesday Book; Walton-le-Dale, the recently discovered site of the Roman Ceccium; Cuerdale, where the immense Danish hoard, comprising above 10,000 Saxon and Danish coins, was discovered; Ribchester, the site of the Roman Rigodunum; Stonyhurst College, once the seat of the ancient Lancashire family of Sherburne, now a noted educational establishment of the Jesuits. Preston, which is open to the saline breezes of the west, is also at a very convenient distance from Lytham, Fleetwood, and Blackpool, with all of which bathing places it is directly connected by rail.

Here we again retrace our journey, and pursue our course from

Crewe to Stockport and Manchester

SANDBACH
Population, 3,252.
Distance from station, 1¼ mile.
Telegraph station at Crewe, 4¾ miles.
Hotel: George.
Market Day: Thursday.
Fairs: Easter Tuesday and Wednesday, and Thursday after Sept. 11th, Dec. 27th.

This is a town occupying a very pretty situation on the banks of the River Wheelock, and embracing within its prospect a panorama that extends from the Welsh mountains in the west, to the Derbyshire hills in the east.

Above: The viaduct in Stockport is still one of the town's outstanding features. Built in 1839, it is over a third of a mile long and consists of twenty-two arches of 63-foot span. At the turn of the twentieth century, 500 trains a day crossed the viaduct.

Left: Stockport Sunday School was mainly erected in 1805 and was the largest Sunday school in the world. There were 100 rooms and two large halls that could accommodate over 3,000 children.

Below: Stockport railway station, platform two southbound, with an LNWR 4-4-0 No. 1417 *Landrail*.

It has no distinct manufacture of its own, but shares in the silk trade to a small extent, whilst being on the verge of the salt region, it derives some additional traffic from that proximity. Lord Crewe is the owner of the place. Its Grammar School is a well-known institution.

There are excellent Brine Springs at Wheelock; St Mary's perpendicular English Church, and a fine old Cross in the Market Place. Abbeyfield, seat of C. Ford, Esq., is in the vicinity.

HOLMES CHAPEL
Population, 573.
Telegraph station at Crewe, 8¼ miles.
Hotel: Swan.
Money Order Office at Middlewich, 4 miles.

Near Bagmere Pool is Brereton Hall, built by Sir W. Brereton, the parliamentary leader.

CHELFORD
Population, 256.
Telegraph station at Stockport, 11¼ miles.
Hotel: Dixon's Arms.
Money Order Office at Knutsford, 4 miles.

Near Chelford are Tatton Park, Lord Egerton; Tabley Hall, Lord de Tabley; Peover Hall, Sir H. Mainwaring, Bart.

ALDERLEY
Population, 1,418.
Telegraph station at Stockport, 8 miles.
Hotel: Queen's.
Money Order Office at Knutsford, 4 miles.
Alderley Park is the seat of Lord Stanley of Alderley.

WILMSLOW
Population, 6,616.
Distance from station, ½ mile.
Telegraph station at Stockport, 6¼ miles.
Hotel: Swan.
Money Order Office at Stockport, 6¼ miles.

Handforth: Cheadle Heath, seat of J. Newton, Esq.

Top left: Manchester Exchange railway station, complete with statue of Oliver Cromwell. The policeman watches the photographer while behind Oliver are the offices of Thomas Cook.

Middle: An unusual visitor to the Old Trafford engine sheds in September 1938 was the Great Northern Railway's No. 1. Designed by Patrick Stirling, this 4-2-2 was built in 1871 at Donacster and had 8-foot-1-inch driving wheels. Designed specifically for London–York expresses, fifty-three were built, with only No. 1 preserved.

Bottom: Bradshaw, a Manchester lad, could hardly have believed that a ship canal would be built to the city but the Manchester Ship Canal could accommodate ships of around 10,000 tons. This view shows the main docks at Salford.

CHEADLE

Population, 6,115.
Telegraph station at Stockport, 2½ miles.
Hotel: White Hart.
Money Order Office at Stockport, 2½ miles.

This is the point of junction with the line to Macclesfield, Congleton, etc. A distance of 2½ miles further brings us to the celebrated Viaduct at Stockport, one of the railway marvels of our time, for it exhibits a roadway actually reared above a populous town, and spanning a valley nearly a third of a mile in length. The height of the parapet above the river Mersey that flows below is 111 feet, and runs on twenty-seven magnificent arches. The cost of the undertaking was upwards of £70,000. It affords the traveller one of the best and most commanding views he can possibly obtain of an English manufacturing town. Thronged streets and narrow lanes stretch out on each side far below; mills and factories rise out of the dense mass of houses, and a forest of chimneys towering upwards, point out the local seats of manufacturing industry. The chief part of the town appears mapped out in bold irregular lines, with the the church of St Mary's crowning the summit; and the view altogether is sufficient to invite curiosity to examine the associations of a place presenting such a busy aspect to the eye.

STOCKPORT

A telegraph station.
Hotel: Warren Bulkeley Arms.

Though greatly improved of late years, Stockport is yet very irregularly built, and the ground on which it stands is remarkable for inequality of surface; from this circumstance, on a winter's night, the numerous and extensive factories elevated above each other, present an appearance when lighted of peculiar and striking grandeur, especially when approached by the high road from the north. It has a population of 54,681, engaged principally in the manufacture of cotton, and returns two members to parliament. The river Mersey divides the town into two unequal parts, the larger portion, that to the south, being situated in Cheshire, and that to the north in Lancashire.

Between fifty and sixty factories are dispersed in and round the town; one of the largest is called Marsland's, a well-known name; it is 300 feet long, and has 600 windows in its six storeys. Others are Howard's, Marshall's, Eskrigge's, etc. Here Radcliffe and Johnson invented the machine for dressing the warp about 1803.

There was a castle here (the site of which is an inn) to guard the ford or port between the two county palatines, on the old Roman road. St Mary's Church, of the fourteenth century, is on a hill. It was restored in 1848; and contains several monumental effigies, etc., of ancient families in the

27

Above: Manchester would eventually have its own dedicated shipping line, the Manchester Liners. Their *Manchester Commerce* is shown here at Salford, *c.* 1910.

Below: At the heart of Manchester is Piccadilly. Woolworth's was originally an American company but the British took it as their own. By 2009, it had gone from the high street, and Manchester, when the company went into receivership.

WOOLWORTH BUILDING, PICCADILLY, MANCHESTER.

neighbourhood. St Thomas's, a large Grecian church, built in 1825. Five bridges cross the Mersey – one of 210 feet span was carried away in the floods of 1798. The Grammar School, founded in 1487, has been rebuilt by Hardwicke; it is under the Goldsmith's Company. The Infirmary is a large neat building, 100 feet long. One pleasing feature of the wholesale manner in which things are done in this part of the world, is an immense Sunday School, built in 1826, 150 or 160 feet wide, and containing eighty-four class rooms. Between 5,000 and 6,000 children are here gathered together on a Sunday to receive religious instruction from pious and devoted volunteers of various denominations. It is endowed with an income of £560.

The Goyt and Etherow, which join the Mersey a little above Stockport, may be ascended to the moorlands, on the Derbyshire border, where the peculiar scenery of the Peak begins. Bramall House, seat of W. Davenport Esq., is a good specimen of the curious and picturesque timber houses, once so common in Lancashire, and Poynton Hall, Lord Vernon's seat, some of whose early ancestors are buried in Stockport Church.

MANCHESTER

Telegraph stations: the Electric and International, Ducie Buildings, Exchange; 1 Mosley Street and at the Railway Stations. The Magnetic and British and Submarine, 11 Ducie Street, Exchange; 19 Bond Street; Queen's Hotel, Portland Street; 36 Thomas Street, Shudehill; Corn Exchange, Hanging Ditch (Thursdays); Lancashire & Yorkshire Railway Stations, Victoria, new Bailey Street, and Oldfield Road; Stock Exchange. The United Kingdom, Bank Street, opposite the Exchange; St Peter's Square.

Hotels: Queen's, Thomas Johnson, first class, for families and gentlemen, recommended. Albion, Palatine and Clarence.

Market Days: Tuesday (manufacturers), Thursday (corn), Friday (manufactures), and Saturday (general). The markets are Victoria, Victoria Street, Smithfield, Shudehill; Bridge Street; London Road. The Cattle Market is in Cross Lane, Salford, held on Tuesdays.

Fairs: Easter Monday and Tuesday, Whit-Monday, Oct. 1st and Nov. 17th.

Races: In Whit-week and September.

Principal Money Order Office: King Street, Manchester.

Bankers: Cunliffes, Brooks & Co.; Heywood Brothers & Co.; Loyd, Entwistle & Co.; James Sewell; the Consolidated, Pall Mall; Branch Bank of England; Manchester and Liverpool District Bank; Manchester and Salford Banking Co.; National Provincial Bank of England; Union Bank of Manchester; Manchester and County.

Manchester, the metropolis of the cotton manufacture, a cathedral city, and parliamentary borough, in the south-east corner of Lancashire, on the Irwell, 188¼ miles from London, and 31½ from Liverpool. The last named town is the real port which supplies its staple article in the raw state, but Manchester

Left: The Mancunian express from London to Manchester.

Middle: No. 9 Dock, Salford, around 1905. The docks were one of the first places in Britain that bananas were regularly imported into. Elders & Fyffes ships would often visit the port, as well as Garston on the Mersey.

Below: At Barton there is a swing bridge over the Manchester Ship Canal, carrying the Bridgewater canal, one of the very first in Britain, over the ship canal.

itself has all the privileges of one, being licensed to bond imported goods as much as if it were by the sea side. It has been the head of a bishop's see since 1848, when a new diocese was taken out of Chester, including the greater part of Lancashire; and the Collegiate Church turned into a cathedral.

Manchester and Salford, though separate boroughs, divided by the Irwell, form one great town, which in 1861 contained a population of 460,428, of which 102,449 belonged to Salford. Manchester returns two members to parliament, and Salford one. With Salford it covers a space of about 3½ miles long, by 2½ broad, and 10 miles in circuit; a line which takes in various suburbs, as Hough, Pendleton, Strangeways, Cheetham, Smedley, Newton, Miles Platting, Beswick, Ardwick, Chorlton-upon-Medlock, Hulme, etc., all of which are continually spreading into the country, and constitute the best built and most modern portion of the town, the most ancient being in the centre, round the Cathedral. The principal buildings of Manchester are not numerous, but scattered; its great features being its vast and busy factories, the industry and spirit of its commercial relations, rather than the display of architectural refinement. But in this respect great changes have already been made; its government possessing a unity of purpose well adapted to develop the various schemes of improvement which from time to time are suggested. The manorial rights, which formerly belonged to the family of the Mosleys, together with the vast surplus profits arising out of the Gas Works, first established in 1817, create a fund calculated to meet the progressive requirements of the times.

Manchester is seated on a wide plain, with a slight elevation here and there; but not far off are the border lines of the three adjacent counties of Yorkshire, Derbyshire, and Cheshire. Some of the most rugged hills and the finest pass scenery in England, may here be witnessed. Four railways traverse this remarkable district – the Lancashire and Yorkshire, London and North Western, Manchester, Sheffield, and Lincolnshire, and South Junction.

Although it was a Roman station under the name of Mancunium, which the Saxons altered to Mancestre, yet there are few remains of antiquity, besides some old timber houses and the College. When Leland undertook his topographical survey in the reign of Henry VIII it was the most populous town in the county, and noted for its woollen goods (even then called cottons), the making of which was introduced by the Flemings of Edward III's time. But about 80 years ago calicoes and cotton muslin began to supersede every other manufacture; Watt's steam-engine, Arkwright's power-loom and factory system, and inexhaustible supplies of coal have given a superiority to Manchester, which it has retained to this day. Within that period it has multiplied its population by seven or eight; and its goods are sent to every corner of the globe. Old people are yet alive who remember the first factory in Miller's Lane, and its great chimney; now there are over 120, a visit to any of which is one of the chief sights of Manchester. Here thread as fine as 460 hanks to the lb. is spun; each hank being 840 yards; and every variety of cotton, silk, and mixed goods, is woven; while, such is the power of production, that cotton may be brought from India, across the sea, made up and shipped again for India, and there sold cheaper than the native dealer can buy it in his own market; while the whole quantity has increased two hundred per cent, the average price has fallen from 7½d to 3½d per yard. It is calculated that, in Lancashire, there are 1,000 factories, with 300,000 hands, and a power of 90,000 horses, moving 1,000,000 power looms and 20,000,000 spindles. Nine-tenths of them are within thirty miles of Manchester. The annual produce is worth £68,000,000 sterling a year, or, one-fourth of a million per day. One half of this is consumed at home.

A piece of cloth, twenty-eight yards long, may be printed in three or four colours in a minute, or nearly one mile of it in an hour. So rapid are the various processes, that goods sent in the grey state from the mill in the afternoon, are bleached, dressed, starched, finished, and placed in the next day's market. Fustians, hats, machines, and locomotive engines, figure among the subordinate branches of manufacture.

Among the factories, notice Birley's, at Chorlton, and Dewhurst's, in the Adelphi, Salford, with its tall stone chimney, 243 feet high, on a base 21 feet square and 45 feet high. The bleach and dye works are placed up and down the Irwell and its tributaries. Wood and Westhead's smallware manufactory, Brook Street; Whitworth's machine factory in Chorlton Street; Sharp's, Atlas Works, Oxford Street; Fairbairn's, in Ancoats; Nasmyth's Bridgewater foundry, at Patricroft, may be visited. Manchester is famed for its magnificent warehouses. For style of architecture and beauty, perhaps Watt's new warehouses in Portland Street, excel all others, and ought by all means to be seen.

Public & Commercial Buildings: After the mills, the chief buildings worth notice are the following: Town Hall, in King Street, built by F. Goodwin, a Grecian colonnade in front, with carved emblems, and a public room under the dome, 130 feet long, ornamented with frescoes. There is a hall for Salford, in Chapel Street: that for Chorlton is in Cavendish Street. Exchange, in Market Street, built 1806 by Harrison, of Chester, is a fine building, with a Doric circular front, which renders the exterior imposing. It has been considerably enlarged and beautified, its area 1,628 square yards, renders it the largest exchange room in Europe. Here may be seen the 'Cotton Lords' on a Tuesday, in their legislative assembly. It contains a portrait, by Lawrence, of T. Stanley, Esq., M.P. Corn Exchange, in Hanging Ditch, built in 1837. The new large Market at Shude Hill (the Manchester Smithfield) should be visited, as its superb glass and iron roof is splendid and unique.

News Rooms, Institutions, Libraries, Places for Recreation, etc.: Royal Institution, in Mosley Street, founded in 1823, and built by Barry, a handsome Grecian building, with a six-column Ionic portico, casts of the Elgin marbles, Chantrey's statue of Dalton, the Manchester chemist, and a lecture theatre; a School of Design forms part of it. Dalton used to lecture at the Literary and Philosophical Society, in George Street, established in 1781. The Manchester Royal School of Medicine and Surgery in Pine Street, founded in 1824;

average number of pupils, 80 to 100. Lectures are given on practical chemistry, anatomy, surgery, etc. Athenæum, in Bond Street, also by Barry; among the pictures is St Francis Xavier, by Murillo; annual literary gatherings are held here, generally presided over by some eminent person. Mechanics' Institution, in David Street, a handsome new building; opened in September, 1856. Free Trade Hall. This fine new edifice, in the pure Italian style of architecture, replaces the large old building in Peter Street, which was without windows, and had no pretensions whatever to architectural display, being principally worthy of notice for the large number of persons it was calculated to hold. It was here, at the first great Anti-Corn Law League Meeting, when the Rev. James William Massie, D.D., had risen to address the assembly that the lights were entirely extinguished, and the vast assembly left in total darkness until the gas could be again lit. The new building is calculated to hold about 7,000 people: its inaugural opening took place on the 8th October, 1856. Portico, a substantial building in Mosley Street, designed by Harrison, of Chester. There are upwards of 14,000 vols. in the library. The files of newspapers are the best out of London. Subscription Concert Hall, Peter Street. Old Subscription Library, Dude Street, founded in 1765, and has 30,000 volumes; the New Library, in the Exchange Buildings, contains 120,000 volumes. Free Library, in a handsomely fitted-up building, in Camp Field (which belonged to the Socialists' body), established at a cost of £12,000, and open to all, young and old, properly recommended. Periodicals and newspapers are supplied in profusion, and there is a library of 21,000 volumes, which are lent out, without restriction. The losses are few, and the privilege is greatly appreciated. First Shakespeare, then Defoe, Scott, and Macaulay, appear, on inquiry, to be the chief favourites with the steady readers. Branch Libraries in Rochdale Road and Hulme. Chatham Library, Chetham's College, contains upwards of 25,000 vols., many of which are rare and valuable. Open to residents and strangers from 10 a.m. to 5 p.m.; during the winter season it closes at 4 p.m. Newall's Buildings Public Library, commenced 1830, 20,000 vols. Foreign Library, St Ann's Street, upwards of 7,000 vols.; French, Italian, German, Spanish, etc. Law Library in Norfolk Street. At Salford, Lark Hill, formerly the residence of the late W. Garnett, Esq., has been converted into a handsome Library and Museum, with the same object as the Free Library at Manchester, with rooms 60 feet to 75 feet long, for reading, pictures, natural history specimens, etc., the sculpture being placed on the broad staircase. The Museum of Natural History in Peter Street contains a good collection. Theatre Royal, in Peter Street, built in 1845, in the modern Italian style, with a fine statue of Shakespeare in front The Queen's, or Minor Theatre, in York Street and Spring Gardens.

Gardens, Parks, etc.: Botanical Gardens, at Old Trafford, a very pretty tract of sixteen acres, with lake, conservatory, etc. Victoria Park, between London and Oxford Roads, is a space of 140 acres, covered with villas. The Queen's Park and museum, on the Rochdale Road , Philip's Park, Bradford Road; and

Left: St Peter's church, Manchester, was consecrated in 1794 and closed its doors on 26 August 1906. It was subsequently demolished.

Below: Belle Vue prison, Gorton, opened in 1850 as a short-term prison for criminals serving less than six months. It closed in 1888 and was demolished in 1892. Belle Vue prison was infamous for the conditions prisoners had to endure.

Peel Park, Salford, are open to the public. Kersal Moor, where the races were held, is now partly cultivated, and has a good church on one part of it.

Colleges, Hospitals, etc.: Lancashire Independent College, established 1840, at Withington. The Wesleyan Theological Institution, Didsbury, opened in 1842, accommodates about forty students for the Wesleyan Ministry. Chetham College, or Blue Coat School, close to the Cathedral, was founded in 1651, by Humphrey Chetham, in the old buildings attached to the Collegiate Church, forming an antique dingy quadrangle, one side of which is appropriated to a library of 25,000 volumes (rarely used), with some curiosities ranged on the walls; and portraits of John Bradford, the martyr (a native of Manchester); Dean Nowell, who compiled the Church Catechism, and others. A statue of the founder, by Theed, was placed in the Cathedral, in 1853. The college is open to the public, and forms an object of attraction. The Grammar School, founded by Bishop Oldham in 1524, and since rebuilt, is near this; it has an income of £4,500. Owen's College, Quay Street; principal, J. G. Greenwood, B.A., founded by John Owen, who bequeathed upwards of £80,000 for the purpose of endowing it. Certificates are issued to candidates for the degrees of bachelor of arts and bachelor of laws, to be conferred by the University of London. The house was formerly the residence of Richard Cobden, Esq., M.P. Chemical laboratory and other conveniences. Commercial Schools, Stretford New Road, built in 1848, by the Manchester Church Educational Society. A library, museum, and specimens of natural history, are attached for the use of the pupils. Ladies' Jubilee School, established in 1806, nearly opposite the Workhouse. In 1832 Mr Francis Hall bequeathed £10,000, which increased the number of pupils to 40, and further improved the building. Other educational and literary societies are the Chetham Society, Natural History Society, Geological Society, Statistical Society, and Manchester Law Association. Royal Infirmary, in Piccadilly, is a large handsome stone building, to which a new dome and portico have been added. It was founded as far back as 1753. It presents a noble appearance. It has six physicians and surgeons, resident surgeons and apothecaries; an income of £9,000, and annually relieves upwards of 20,000 patients (see *Bradshaw's Hand-book to the Manufacturing Districts*). Bronze statues of the Duke of Wellington, Sir Robert Peel, Watt, and Dalton, adorn the grounds in front of the institution. It is intended to add one of Her Majesty. School for the Deaf and Dumb, and Henshaw's Blind Asylum, are near the Botanical Gardens, at Old Trafford, with a chapel serving for both, all in a handsome Tudor style, with a front 280 feet long. Lane was the architect, in 1836. Lunatic Asylum at Prestwich.

Prisons, Workhouses, etc.: New Assize Courts, Strangeways. The City Gaol, at Hyde Road, commenced in 1847, completed in 1849, employing 200 workmen, and using ten million bricks, capable of holding about 432 prisoners, carried on upon the solitary system. It is enclosed by a boundary wall 20 feet high, and 2 feet 8 inches thick, and consists of three wings for male prisoners, and one for females, and one (the shortest) contains

Above: Royal visits were a relatively common occurrence in Manchester. The LNWR had its own special Royal Train, which had been built at Wolverton. This view shows the Royal Train with King Edward VII aboard at Bredbury on 12 July 1905.

Middle and below: In 1921, the Prince of Wales visited Manchester on 7 July. Part of the crowd are waiting to give him a hearty welcome on the photo above. The Lord Mayor's Daimler limousine leads the procession of vehicles from Exchange station.

the chapel, hospital, etc. The New Bailey Prison, on the Salford side of the Irwell, was begun in 1787, in Howard's time, who laid the first stone; it is an extensive range, with nearly six hundred cells in it, besides wards, work-rooms, sessions-house, police-court, etc. A high wall, surrounded by an iron chevaux de frise encloses the whole; turrets at the angles of the building, with loop holes for firing through, are placed for defence in case of attack. Holds 583 males, and 214 females. Union Poor-House, erected in 1792, at a cost of about £30,000, in New Bridge Street, Strangeways, is a little town in itself, capable of accommodating upwards of 1,000 persons. The New Workhouse and Farm at Crumpsall, having about fifty acres of land attached to it, which furnishes employment for a considerable number of able bodied poor. At Swinton, four miles on the Bolton Road, on a site of thirty-four acres, is a large branch Industrial School, in the Elizabethan style, by Tattersall and Dickson, with room for 1,500 pauper children. The Salford Workhouse is in Eccles New Road, that for Chorlton-upon-Medlock at Withington.

Barracks: Cavalry Barracks, Chester Road, accommodates upwards of 300 men and horses, besides commissioned and non-commissioned officers, etc. Infantry Barracks, Regent Road, Salford, will hold above 700 men, besides officers.

Railway Stations: London and North Western, London Read and Victoria; Manchester, Sheffield, and Lincolnshire, London Road; Lancashire and Yorkshire, Victoria, Hunt's Bank, and New Bailey Street, Salford; South Junction and Altrincham, Oxford Road and Knott Mill.

Bridges: Several bridges, of short dimensions, cross the Irwell and its two branches, the Irk and Medlock, the best of which is the Victoria Bridge, a noble stone arch, 100 feet span, near the Cathedral; rebuilt in 1839, in place of the old Gothic bridge of the time of Edward III. That at Broughton (uniting Broughton with Pendleton) is a very handsome suspension bridge, which had the misfortune to fall in while a detachment of soldiers were passing over it some years ago, but since rebuilt. Other bridges are the Blackfriars, at the end of St Mary's Gate; Albert Bridge (late New Bailey), near the prison; Regent Road; Dude; Springfield Lane; The Iron Bridge, New Bridge Street; and Broughton (uniting Salford with Broughton); at the latter tolls are taken, as also at the suspension. A new bridge from Water Street to Ordeal Lane. In Fairfield Street, on the Birmingham line, is one of the best Skew Bridges in the kingdom, by Buck; it is at an angle of 24° only, built of iron, 128 feet span, six-ribbed, and weighing 540 tons: the width of the street is only 48 feet.

Churches and Chapels: The Cathedral, originally a collegiate church, founded by the Delawarrs, is a handsome perpendicular English cross. A great variety of grotesque carvings are seen without and in the choir; the roof is flat, but adorned with fretwork. There are several chapels, formerly the chantries of the Trafford, Stanley, and other families, of whom it contains some monumental brasses. Theed's statue of Chetham is here. Few of the other churches deserve notice. At St Peter's, is a picture of the Descent from

Left: Manchester Victoria is the second-busiest station in Manchester, after Piccadilly. It still serves Liverpool on the old Liverpool & Manchester Railway line, the first intercity railway in the world.

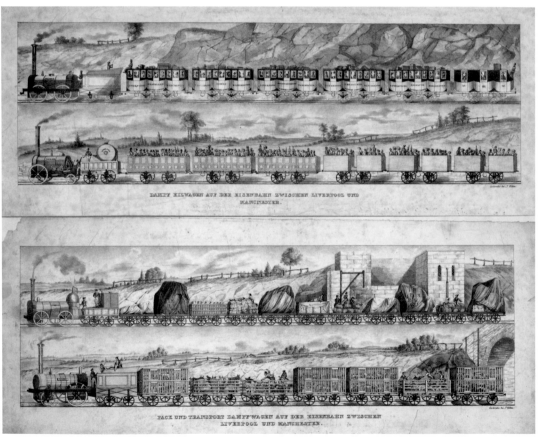

DAMPF EILWAGEN AUF DER EISENBAHN ZWISCHEN LIVERPOOL UND MANCHESTER.

PACK UND TRANSPORT DAMPFWAGEN AUF DER EISENBAHN ZWISCHEN LIVERPOOL UND MANCHESTER.

Above: From a German publication of the 1830s, these views show typical trains on the original Liverpool & Manchester Railway, which opened in 1830, kick-starting the railway revolution that would see George Bradshaw branch out from his canal maps into railway guide publishing.

the Cross, by G. Caracci. Near this church was the field of 'Peterloo', where the celebrated reform meeting, called by Henry Hunt, the blacking maker, was dispersed by the yeomanry, in 1819, with the loss of several lives. St Matthew's large church stands on the site of the Roman station, or Castle Field. There are altogether about fifty churches and chapels. The Roman Catholics possess two or three handsome chapels, the best being their Cathedral, at Salford, which is 200 feet long, with a handsome west front, and spire 240 feet high.

Cemeteries: Rusholme Road, Ardwick, Harpurhey, Cheetham Hill (Wesleyan), and the Salford Borough Cemetery, in the Eccles New Road.

Clubs: Union, Mosley Street; Albion, King Street.

Of two well-known chemists, Henry was a native, and Dalton here developed his great discovery of the Atomic theory, which has done so much to give precision to the science. Among the living natives are Ainsworth, the novelist, and two poets, C. Swain and T. K. Hervey.

In the neighbourhood is Heaton Park, the seat of the Earl of Wilton, modernised by Wyatt.

London and North Western continued
Manchester to Liverpool

VICTORIA STATION

Although not strictly speaking the first railway in England, the Liverpool and Manchester line was really the first on which was attempted the practical application of locomotive power for the transit of goods and passengers, and it is, therefore, preeminently entitled to rank as the pioneer of those stupendous undertakings which have not only given a new stimulus to the mechanical and architectural genius of the age, but have enabled this country to take the lead of all others in these respects, not less than in manufactures. Important as were the direct objects proposed by the original projectors of this line, of bringing the vast district of our manufacturing industry within an hour's distance of the port where its staple material, and the supplies of food were landed, and whence its fabrics were exported to the ends of the earth, the result is, after all, the lowest in the scale. England has since developed her resources to an extent which, at the time of its trial, would have appeared incredible, and in the space of comparatively a few years, the whole island has been intersected by this new class of roads, as much superior to the old highways, as were those of the Roman conquerors to the tangled forest paths of our Celtic ancestors.

The first and greatest work on this portion was the immense bog of Chat Moss, which comprised an area of twelve square miles, varying in depth from 10 to 35 feet, consisting of sixty million tons of vegetable matter, of so soft and spongy a texture that cattle could not walk over it. Those who are now whirled over this once trackless waste, the numerous viaducts and embankments, and along the immense excavations of the remainder of the line, can with difficulty appreciate the amount of skill, perseverance, and labour expended in works that are now concealed from general observation. Other lines, too, have been formed under immense difficulties, which have been surmounted by the inventive genius and indomitable energies of our engineers; but it must ever be remembered, that in the accomplishment of this line, every portion of the work was an experiment, and that the engineers and proprietors, virtually, and at their own cost, supplied the civilized world, not only with the initiatory example, but with an invaluable amount of information and experience acquired in the construction, progress, and management of this—the acknowledged model of every succeeding railway.

ORDSAL LANE and WEASTE stations.

ECCLES

Telegraph station at Manchester, 4 miles.

Hotel: Bull's Head.

This little village is prettily situated on the northern banks of the Irwell, and environed by some of the most picturesque rambles; one of which, along the side of the river, about two miles up the stream, leads to a ferry by which the tourist may get ready access to Trafford Park.

The place is celebrated for its cakes, also for its old church, which belonged to Whalley Abbey, and gives name (Ecclesia) to the parish. It has some monuments of the Booths and Breretons. At the vicarage the Right Honourable William Huskisson expired after his lamentable accident on the opening of the railway. Cotton and silk are woven here.

PATRICROFT

Telegraph station at Manchester, 5 miles.

Here is Nasmyth's celebrated foundry, the largest in England.

A short walk from this station, along the canal, brings us to Worsley Hall, the seat of the Earl of Ellesmere, where Queen Victoria was so nobly entertained on the occasion of her visit to Manchester in 1851. The present splendid mansion was rebuilt by Blore in 1846, in the Elizabethan style of architecture. The late earl inherited the vast estates of the celebrated Duke of Bridgewater, for whom Brindley, the engineer, first made the subterranean canals here. They supply the coal mines below at a depth of 180 feet, and wind in and out for 18 miles. Landseer's well-known Return from Hawking may be seen at the house; and in the neighbourhood are a few of the timber and plaster buildings formerly so common in this part of England. One of them, Peel Hall, the seat of Lord Kenyon; was built in 1630, and has a great number of old rooms and portraits. From the park you get a view of Leigh and the Cheshire hills.

From Patricroft, a run of about 10 minutes brings us past Barton Moss and Astley.

Bury Lane, the commencement of Chat Moss, and Kenyon, the junction of the line to Bolton, are soon left behind, and we reach

Parkside, a place memorable by the death of W. Huskisson, Esq., the celebrated statesman, on the opening of the line, September 15th, 1830. A tablet is placed here in commemoration of the event.

NEWTON

Population 5,903. A telegraph station.

Hotel: Legh Arms.

Here the Highlanders were defeated, in 1648. M'Corquodale & Co.'s printing works should be visited. In the vicinity are Castle Hill, with its old oaks, and Haydock Park, seat of T. Legh, Esq., used as a private Lunatic Asylum, under the direction of Mr. Sutton.

WARRINGTON JUNCTION, COLLINS GREEN, AND ST HELENS JUNCTION

St Helens to Warrington, Runcorn, and Liverpool

From St Helens Junction the line diverges to the left, passing the stations of Peasley Cross, Sutton, Clock Face, Farnworth, and Appleton, en route to Runcorn Gap. By means of a ferry across the river we reach

RUNCORN

Noted as one of the inland ports of the kingdom, and much resorted to for bathing in the summer season. Population, 10,434.

From Runcorn Gap the railway again diverges to the right, and after passing the stations of Fidler's Ferry and Sankey Bridges, we arrive at Warrington.

We again return to Runcorn Gap, and in pursuing our journey towards Liverpool, pass the stations of Ditton, Halewood, and Speke, arriving at

GARSTON

The present terminus of the railway. Population, 4,720.

A telegraph station.

In the vicinity are Allerton Hall, the old seat of Roscoe, the historian, and Woolton Hall, a fine edifice, built by Adam, near which is the site of an old priory and a camp.

The rest of the journey, about six miles, is performed by omnibuses.

Above: The four views above show the interiors of the coaches of the American Special from Euston to Liverpool Riverside station. With Liverpool being the base for so many transatlantic customers, it was important to get passengers and mail to and from London as quickly as possible, and so the luxury expresses were sent in conjunction with the ship departures and arrivals. These views are typical of First Class aboard the expresses, with their special coaches, which included everything from smoking saloons to dining cars. Every luxury was catered for, including afternoon tea in the saloon de luxe.

Left: The old Landing Stage at Liverpool, *c.* 1870. Princes Landing Stage had been constructed in the 1850s and was designed to float so as to cope with the tides of the Mersey.

London and North Western continued

St Helens Junction to Liverpool

From St Helen's Junction the line passes the stations of Lea Green, Rainhill, Huyton Quarry, Huyton, Roby, and Broad Green, when, soon after, the train stops at

EDGEHILL

Here the traveller sees before him a dark, yawning aperture, which, for the few minutes he is delayed, may excite a temporary imagining as to his probable destination. When informed, however, that this tunnel literally pierces into the very heart of Liverpool, burrowing beneath streets thickly tenanted by the suburban population, and constantly conducting trains freighted with hundreds of travellers like himself; under the surface of a region animated by a mighty multitude, intent upon the pursuits of everyday life, he may feel inclined to pay a just tribute to the engineering skill of those who were enabled to propose and complete a work of such kind in the early days of railway history. This tunnel is one mile and a quarter in length; but the one which conveys the merchandise to Wapping, near the King's Dock, is still longer; and a third tunnel, for the conveyance of goods to the North Docks, has also been constructed.

Arrived at the station at Lime-street, the passenger will find it worth his while to bestow a glance at its architecture, its peculiar adaptation to all the requirements of an extensive railway system being best exhibited by the superior accommodation enjoyed by the public, and the regularity with which all the official duties are performed. The building is in the Italian style, presenting a columnar and pilastered front, with four arches for the admission of vehicles, etc.

LIVERPOOL

Telegraph stations, 35, Castle Street, 9, Exchange Buildings, and at the Lime Street Railway Station.

Bankers: Israel Barned and Co.; A. Heywood, Sons, and Co.; Leyland and Bullins; Moss and Co.; Bank of Liverpool; Branch Bank of England; Liverpool Commercial Banking Company; Branch Manchester and Liverpool District Banking Company; North and South Wales Bank; Royal Bank, Liverpool; Liverpool Union Bank; J. E. Kneeshaw; Edwin L. Samuel; Alliance Bank of London & Liverpool.

Hotels: Victoria, and London North and Western Railway Hotel, opposite St George's Hall, a most comfortable house, and much commended. Radley's Adelphi; Lynn's Waterloo, Ranelagh Street.

Omnibuses to and from the station. Market Days: Daily.

Fairs: Every alternate Wednesday, beginning March 12th, July 25th, Nov. 11th.

Races: (At Aintree) in February, July, and November.

Top left: Brunel's *Great Eastern* was well known to the compilers of *Bradshaw's Guide.* After all, it was the biggest ship in the world and was almost new when the guide was published. The ship was a failure and was broken up on the Mersey. One of her masts remains at Anfield, as the flagpole.

Left: By the twentieth century the docks in Liverpool were among the largest in Britian, second only to London. Ships of Cunard, White Star, Blue Funnel, Blue Star, American Line, Canadian Pacific, Elders & Fyffes, Anchor, Allan and Dominion were just some of the vessels calling on a daily basis.

Below: St George's Hall, Liverpool, in the 1890s.

The Lyrpool, or Litherpool, of early times, when it was an insignificant chapelry, sent one little bark with six men to the siege of Calais, in 1338, Hastings then sending twenty-one tall ships, but is now the second port in the United Kingdom, as well as a parliamentary borough, etc., with a population of 375,955, who return two members. It stands fronting the Irish Sea on the north side of the Mersey's mouth, at the south extremity of Lancashire, 210 miles from London, by the North Western Railway, via Warrington; 230 miles by way of Birkenhead and Chester; and as near as can be in the centre of the British Islands. The site a sloping rock of red sandstone, through which three tunnels are cut from the Edge Hill Station – one to the Lime Street terminus (opposite St George's Hall), another for goods, of 1¼ mile long, to Wapping, and a third, as long, to Clarence Dock. The Mersey, above the town, widens into a little shallow sea, 2 miles wide in one part; while at the mouth it is choked by large sandbanks, leaving two main entrances – the Victoria Channel, 12 miles long, the most used – and the Rock Channel, 10 miles in length. Besides the Floating Light House off New Brighton, like the Eddystone, and 90 feet high.

The Docks, which are the grand lions of the town, extend in one magnificent range of 5 miles along the river, from Toxteth Park to Kirkdale; the newer ones being near the latter suburb, to the north, and most of them constructed since 1845. All steamers can enter (except some of the very largest), which are obliged to anchor in the river. The Collingwood, one of the finest docks in this quarter, is 500 yards long and 160 wide, and covers a space of 131 acres. Clarence dock to the south of these, is of an older date. Prince's dock is also 500 yards long and chiefly used by American liners. At George's dock, in front of St Nicholas' Church, is the new Floating Pier, whence steamers run to various points of the river. Canning dock, since it was altered, is 500 yards long, including what was the old dock. Albert dock was opened in 1845, by Prince Albert, with warehouses surrounding it, on the London plan – the usual practice at Liverpool being to build warehouses separate from the docks. Passing the tobacco, timber, salt, and other docks, you come to that called the Herculaneum, at the south end of the chain. Altogether the twenty-one docks have 15 miles of quay room, will hold 1,500 sail, and enclose 200 acres of water. The dock dues in 1849 were £224,000; the tonnage in 1846 belonging to the port was 390,000, while the total tonnage trading inwards and outwards exceeded that of London. Customs, however, were only £3,620,000, while London was 11 millions. In the same year the exports of all kinds were valued at 28½ millions sterling; the imports from Ireland alone were 8 millions. These numbers may serve to give an idea of the extent of its commercial relations. To this we may add that nearly 2 million bales of raw cotton are imported for the staple supply of the factories dispersed through Lancashire – a wonderful quantity compared with the little bag which a private firm sent from America in 1785, as a venture, along with other goods. Liverpool, as might be expected, is a great emigrant port. As many as 206,000, for whose use half a million tons of shipping were

Left: Liverpool is famous not just for its docks but also for having the first intercity railway between the city and Manchester. Designed and planned to carry freight between the docks and Manchester, it soon became apparent that passengers would quickly be the largest revenue generator for the railway. No longer could the time taken to travel 20 miles be counted in days, but in hours, and soon it would be in minutes.

Below: A test of numerous engines was made at Rainhill in 1829, the successful winner of which was George and Robert Stephenson's *Rocket*, the first truly modern locomotive. *Rocket* is now in the Science Museum, but is shown here with LNWR No. 2155 *W.C. Brocklehurst* at Crewe in November 1910. While *Rocket* survives, no George the Fifth locomotives have been preserved.

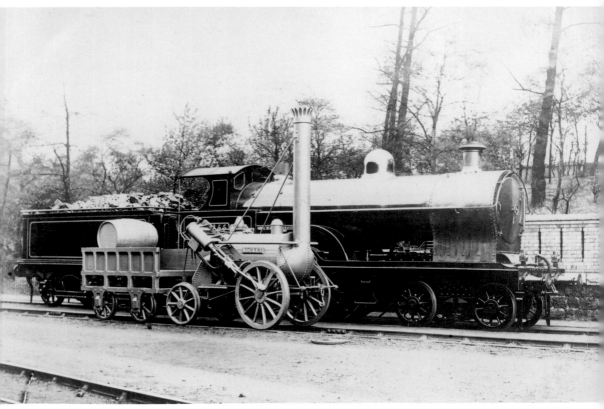

required, started in 1851. A large Home has been built near the docks for their accommodation. The shipbuilding establishments of Messrs Rennie Co. – Jordan and Getty – Cato and Miller – Steel and Challoner – and Laird's, Clayton and Kereven, and Glover and Royle's on the Birkenhead side, are particularly worth inspecting.

The town covers a space of 7 to 8 square miles; Castle, Lord, Bold, and other streets near the docks are the most bustling; Rodney, Parliament, and Shaw Streets, the best built. The public buildings are – the Collegiate Institution, designed by H. Elmes, in Shaw Street, built in 1843, in the Tudor style, 300 feet long. The magnificent establishment lately erected in Church Street, by Messrs. Elkington and Co. The Town Hall, at one end of Castle Street, is a handsome pile, by J. Foster, on a rustic base, with a portico of four columns, and under an open dome, built in 1795. Lawrence's portrait of George III, and Chantrey's statue of Canning are here. In the Exchange quadrangle behind is Westmacott's statue of Nelson. At the other end of Castle Street is the Custom House, a very extensive building, also by Foster, with a dome and four Ionic porticoes, in one of which is a statue of Huskisson. It occupies the site of the first dock cut at Liverpool, in 1699. The Post Office and other offices are collected under this roof. Close to this is the new Sailors' Home, a striking building in the Italian style, built in 1850, 190 feet long, with turrets at the corners, and full of windows.

There are excellent libraries at the Athenæum and Lyceum news rooms, which represent the two great political parties in the town; the former is in Bold Street, and the latter in Church Street. New Music Hall, 175 feet long, in Hope Street, built in 1849. St John's Market, in Elliott Street, was built in 1812, by Foster, and is 560 feet long; it covers two acres, intersected by five walks, and is a scene of extraordinary bustle on market days. The Theatre is in Williamson Square, near the Amphitheatre, both of good size. It was on the stage of the former that the celebrated actor, Palmer, died in 1798, after uttering the words, 'there is another and a better world'. Large Poor House, on Brownlow Hill, near the Lunatic Asylum, and the Infirmary – the latter built by Foster, with a six column portico.

The best building, and perhaps the finest in all England, is St George's Hall, opposite Lime Street Railway Station. It was originally designed by H. Elmes, a very promising young architect, since dead. Its dimensions are 600 feet by 170, surrounded by Grecian columns of truly magnificent proportions, including assize and other courts. The building was began in 1841, and was opened by Her Majesty in 1855; it cost about £200,000. Many of its decorations and exterior approaches are still incomplete. The Public Hall is 180 feet long and 84 high, with a marble floor, and a vaulted roof of hollow bricks. The Concert Room will hold 1,400 persons. The Nisi Prius and Crown Courts form a half circle, 60 feet by 50, with an arched-paneled ceiling, resting on granite pillars. There are sixteen fluted pillars in the east portico, 40 feet high, on a flight of steps 200 feet long. In the south portico are eight pillars, and Gibson's statue of George Stephenson. The basement is ventilated by small airholes along the floor line.

St James' Cemetery is a really attractive spot, in Upper Duke Street, laid out in an old quarry, with catacombs, and a mausoleum containing Gibson's statue of Huskisson, the statesman, who represented Liverpool when he was killed at the opening of the railway to Manchester, in 1830. The Necropolis Cemetery is in the Everton Road. The Mechanics Institution, in Mount Street, is in fact an excellent school, established in 1835, by the liberal party, previous to the Collegiate Institution, which was set up by the conservatives. Lord Brougham laid the foundation stone. In Colquitt Street is the Royal Institution School, founded by Roscoe; with a gallery of marbles and casts (among others, the Panhellenium casts, the only ones in England). Romney's cartoons, Gibson's (of his falling angels); and a museum, (Roscoe's portrait is here; he lived when a youth at Mount Pleasant, and published his Lorenzo de Medici at Liverpool). Blue Coat School is behind Church Street. Blind school (oldest in England) in Hardman Street; Hilton's 'Christ giving sight to the blind' is here. The baths and washhouses in Frederick Street, opened June, 1842, were the first of the kind erected in England.

Churches and Chapels: Eighty-five altogether, of which forty belong to the establishment. Liverpool forms one parish, with two rectors. St Nicholas, the mother church, is near the docks, and has Gibson's monument of Mr Earle, a tower and lantern, rebuilt in 1810, with the bells of St Selsher's, Winford, presented by Cromwell; the first church here dates back to 1361 and held a favourite shrine to the patron saint of seamen. St Peter's, the other parish church, is a plain building. St Luke's, at the top of Bold Street, is a very handsome imitation of the Gothic style, finished in 1831, from Foster's designs, at a cost of £44,000. St George's, or the corporation church, in Castle Street, which stands on the site of a castle, begun by Henry II, which came to the Stanleys and Molyneuxs, is also by Foster. St Michael's, in Kent Street, has a steeple 200 feet high. That of St Martin's, in Scotland Road, is as high, Gothic, by Foster. Everton Church, on a hill, has a conspicuous tower, 340 feet above the river. It was here that Prince Rupert fixed his head-quarters in the siege of 1644. It is a great place for toffy. St Paul's, in Prince's Park, is a fine modern Gothic church, built for Dr M. Neile, in 1850, with a tall spire. The park covers forty acres, with a lake, villas, etc., round it. Near this is a pretty green spot called the Dingle, opening to the river. Among the Chapels are, Dr Raffles', in George Street; the original one was rather a handsome building, oval within, the seats rising towards the wall, built in 1811, but since burnt, and the present one erected on its site. Baptist Chapel, in Myrtle Street, Roman Catholic Chapels of St Nicholas, in Blake Street, and St Anthony, in Scotland Road. Unitarian Chapel, in Hope Street, with Thorwaldsen's relief. All these are in the Gothic style.

In the vicinity of the town are the Botanic Gardens, on a site of eleven acres; the Cattle Market, at Stanley; the Sessions House, at Kirkdale, near the Industrial School for 1,150 children; New Church, in a decorated English style, at Fairfield, with a tower of 147 feet; and Mr. Lascelles' Observatory, where a satellite of Neptune, and an additional one of Saturn, have been discovered. The Dock Observatory, under Mr Hartnup, is a red granite tower, having a 12-foot equatorial telescope, etc.

Legh Richmond was born in St Paul's Square, and Mrs Hemans, in Duke Street. Gibson, one of the greatest living sculptors, though not a native, is best known here by some of his choicest productions. Mr R. Yates has his Cupid and Butterfly; Mrs Sandbach, his Greek Hunter and Aurora; Mr Elmes, his Sappho.

Within a few miles of Liverpool are the following: Bootle, Waterloo, and Southport, bathing places on the coast of the Irish Sea. Scarisbrick, C. Scarisbrick, Esq.; here are pictures by J. Martin, who died in 1854. Knowsley, Earl of Derby, in a large park, which till lately contained a valuable museum of natural history, and menagerie (the greater portion of which was collected by that indefatigable, scientific, and learned botanist, Dr Thomas Whitfield, during a long residence at Sierra Leone, where his gratuitous medical aid to the Western Africans has deeply endeared him to all classes of natives and Europeans); part of which was bequeathed to the people of Liverpool. The Stanley portraits are here, from the first Earl, Henry VII's father-in-law. Croxteth Park, Earl of Sefton, the seat of the Molyneux family; the house is in part ancient. Wavertree, a pretty country village, with part of an ancient well at the pond, dated 1414. At Childwall, belonging to the Marquis of Salisbury, are some remains of a priory. Allerton was the seat of Roscoe, in his prosperous days, where he lived happy with his books, which he so feelingly laments parting with:

> Loved associates, chiefs of elder art!
> Teachers of wisdom, who could once beguile
> My tedious hours, and brighten every toil.

Here Gibson, then a youth, used to visit him. Hale, seat of J. Blackburne, Esq., was the birth place of a giant, called the Child of Hale, 9½ feet in height. Hazles, Sir T. Birch, Bart. Prescot is a thriving town for pottery, watch tools, files, etc., at the west corner of the great coal field. John Kemble was born here in 1757. At St Helens are large and old established plate glass works.

The Cheshire side of the Mersey is now a prosperous suburb of Liverpool, with a softer climate and more attractive scenery. Birkenhead is a growing port, with a floating dock formed by Wallasey Pool, of 150 acres. It has two or three handsome churches, a vast square of six acres, market-house, and some fragments of a priory of the 12th century. It has also a public park, certainly not one of the largest, but, as a model, allowed to be one of the finest in England. Bidston Hill and lighthouse are behind; and Stourton Quarry, in which ripple marks have been discovered by geologists. Rod

Left: While the original West Coast Main Line was purely an LNWR route, by 1923, with the railway amalgamations of that year, it was possible to travel on a single line, the London, Midland & Scottish from Euston, via Manchester and onwards on the Lancashire & Yorkshire to Bolton and points north. The Lancashire & Yorkshire had a works at Horwich, on the outskirts of Manchester.

Middle left: Bolton was once a major manufacturing town and where the spinning mule was invented by Samuel Crompton. Arkwright also lived here. These two views show Deansgate, one of the major streets of Bolton.

Below: Two Bolton Corporation trams cross paths near Horwich on 27 April 1938.

Ferry, Bromborough, and Eastham, up the river, are charming spots. Hooton Halt belongs to J. Naylor, Esq. This part of Cheshire is called the Wirral.

Hoylake: This place is approached from Birkenhead by omnibus; it is a quiet watering place at the mouth of the Dee.

New Brighton: Hotel, Victoria, first class; distance from Liverpool, by steamer, 6 miles; or from Birkenhead, by hired conveyance, 5 miles. It is a very pleasant watering place on the Cheshire side of the Mersey, and derives its chief interest from the beautiful panorama which the shipping on the river constantly affords. Excursions may be made to Leasowe Castle, Birkenhead Park, Eastham, etc.

The facility and cheapness of steam transit, either by rail or boat, gives the tourist an excellent opportunity of making Liverpool the starting point to some delightful spots on the Welsh coast. During the summer months there is daily steam communication between Menai Bridge, Bangor, Beaumaris, and Liverpool. The passage is accomplished in about five hours.

Another route for those who like to enjoy the country by occasionally pedestrianising, is to take the packet from Liverpool to Rhyl, or Mostyn, North Wales, and thence continue the journey on foot, or the line of railway from Chester to Holyhead, which affords the same facilities for reaching picturesque stations.

LANCASHIRE AND YORKSHIRE

Manchester, Bolton, and Liverpool

SALFORD (Oldfield Road)
A telegraph station.
Market Days: Saturday and Tuesday (cattle).
Fairs: Whit Monday, and November 17th.

This is a borough town, joining Manchester, with a population of 102,499, who return one member. Its principal buildings are St John's cruciform Roman Cathedral, by Weightman, 200 feet by 130, with a spire 240 feet; the west front is a facsimile of Howden Church, York. The Town Hall, Market Place, by Goodwin, House of Correction, Barracks, Schools, Trinity Church, built in 1634, Library, Lying-in Hospital, Dorcas Society, print works and factories. In the vicinity is Kersall Moor; here the troops were encamped in 1848. Byron the poet and stenographer was a native of Kersall Cell, the seat of Miss Atherton.

PENDLETON
A telegraph station.

This is a populous place, and contains 20,900 inhabitants, employed in the cotton trade.

51

Passing Clifton (the Junction of the Line to Bury, etc.), Dixon Fold, Stoneclough, Halshaw Moor, and Moses Gate, we arrive at

BOLTON-LE-MOORS

A telegraph station.

Hotel: Swan.

Market Days: Monday and Saturday.

Fairs: Jan. 4th, July 30th and 31st, Oct. 13th and 14th, cattle; and every other Monday.

Bankers: Bank of Bolton; Hardcastle, Cross, and Company.

A large manufacturing town, on the moors, where five or six railways meet. Population, 70,395, who send two members to parliament. Cotton velvets and muslins were first manufactured here about 1760–80, on a large scale, by the new machinery of Arkwright, who resided here when a barber; and Crompton, who lived at Hall-in-the-Wood, an old timbered house, (when a weaver, and there invented the mule). It was the Starkies' old seat, and still exists. Long before the cotton trade took root, Bolton was a great place for cloth and fustians, the making of which was introduced by the Flemings in 1337. There are now sixty cotton mills, many of them very large, as are also the bleach and dye-works, the whole employing about 13,000 hands. Muslins, counterpanes, cambrics, dimity, ginghams, etc, are the chief productions. Above 4,000 hands are engaged in the iron foundries and engine works. Much coal is quarried, and a little paper made.

Among the buildings are the old Parish Church, Town Hall, Free Library, Public Baths, Infirmary, Church Institute for elementary education, Market Hall, the finest in England, opened in Dec. 1855, cost about £80,000; large Waterworks supplied by reservoirs 4 miles distant, Exchange, Theatre, Foundries, Mechanics' Institute, Lever's Grammar School, where the lexicographer Ainsworth was both pupil and master. At Dobson's machine works is an immense brick chimney, 363 feet high. At one time the manor belonged to the Derby family, and it was here that the loyal seventh Earl was brought to be beheaded in 1651, after his defeat at Wigan Lane. His Countess, who defended Lathom House so heroically against the roundheads, a few years before, was the Charlotte de Tremouaille who figures in 'Peveril of the Peak'. Smithills Hall contains a chapel, with stained window and curious old carvings, and is the seat of the Ainsworths, near their bleach-works at Halliwell.

Two miles distant is Eagley, with Messrs Chadwick's sewing thread and smallware mills, most admirably arranged in every respect; adjacent is a school, with pleasure grounds and excellent library containing the daily papers for the use of the work-people, whose happiness and comfort have been most carefully attended to by those spirited and philanthropic gentlemen.

BOLTON AND KENYON

Passing Daubhill, Chequerbent (near which is Hulton Park, the seat of W. Hulton, Esq.), Atherton, we arrive at

LEIGH

A telegraph station.
Hotel: White Horse.
Market Day: Saturday.
Fairs: April 5th and 24th; Dec 7th and 8th.

A market town, with a population of 10,621, who are employed in the cambric, muslin and fustian trades. The pasture land is good, and coal and limestone abound in the neighbourhood. Cheese is made here. Hight, the original inventor of the spinning jenny and water frame, which Arkwright only improved, was a native.

We then pass Bradshaw Leach, and arrive at Kenyon, the junction of the lines to Liverpool and Manchester.

Bolton to Wigan and Liverpool

LOSTOCK JUNCTION

Bolton to Preston

Passing Lostock Junction, Lostock Lane, Blackrod, with its sulphur spring, and Adlington stations, we arrive at

CHORLEY

A telegraph station.
Hotel: Royal Oak.
Market Day: Tuesday.
Fairs: March 26th, May 5th, August 20th, and September 4th and 6th.

This is a market town, with a population of 15,013, engaged in the cotton trade, and working the coal, lead, and slate mines. Here is St Laurence's Church, with its old monuments, St George's, built in the Gothic style in 1825, and an excellent Grammar School. In the vicinity are Astley Hall, Lady Highten, Gillibrand Hall, H. Fazakerley, Esq., and the Bleaching Works, which are well worth a visit.

Passing close to Euxton Hall, the seat of W. Anderton, Esq., Shaw Hall, and Cuerden Park, we reach Euxton, Leyland, and Farington stations.

Preston to Oxenholme

Passing Broughton and Brock stations, at the latter of which is Claughton Hall, built in Charles I's time, but now a farm, and stone quarries in the neighbourhood, we reach

GARSTANG

Distance from station, 2 miles.
Telegraph station at Preston, 9¼ miles.
Hotel: Royal Oak.
Market Day: Thursday.
Fairs: Holy Thursday, July 10th, and Dec. 22nd.

A market town situated on the Wyre, with a population of 714, employed in the cotton and print trade. It contains town hall, free school, print and cotton factories, four chapels, and a church, rebuilt in 1746. In the river is good trout and chub fishing; close by are the remains of Greenhalgh Castle, which was garrisoned by the Earl of Derby for Charles I in 1643. The Pretender occupied this place in 1715. In the vicinity are Kirkland Hall, seat of T. Cole, Esq.; Bleasdale Tower, seat of W. J. Garnett, Esq., M.P., and Bleasdale Fell, 1,709 feet high.

Passing Scorton station, we arrive at Bay Horse. In the vicinity are Ellel Grange, seat of W. Preston, Esq.; Thurnham Hall, the Daltons' seat, and Ashton Hall on the Lune, the finely wooded park and princely seat of Le Gendre N. Starkie, Esq. (formerly of the Duke of Hamilton), which commands an extensive view of the Irish Sea.

Passing Galgate station, we reach

LANCASTER

A telegraph station.
Hotels: King's Arms and Royal Hotel; Joseph Sly. See Household Words, Nos. 395 and 396, October 1857, where this hotel is noticed in the following terms: 'The order was promptly executed (truly, all orders were so, in that excellent hotel).' We can certainly endorse this remark of Mr Dickens.
Market Days: Wednesday and Saturday.
Fairs: May 1st to 3rd, July 5th to 7th, August 11th to 13th, and Oct. 10th, three days each, first day for cattle, second for cheese, and third for toys.
Races: In July.
Bankers: Lancaster Banking Co.; Branch of Preston Banking Co.

Lancaster, capital of Lancashire, a parliamentary borough (two members), and port, with a population of 16,005, engaged in the cotton trade, and a small coasting trade, at the mouth of the Lune, near Glasson Dock. From its Saxon name, Loncastre, meaning the camp or fortress on the Lune, it is likely there was a Roman station, but this is an unsettled point. Subsequent to the Conquest, it was the head of a crown manor which, in the person of Edward III's son, John of Gaunt, 'time-honoured Lancaster', as Shakespeare styles him, was created a duchy, with a separate jurisdiction, which exists to this day, the Chancellorship of the Duchy of Lancaster being a ministerial office, while the dukedom is held by the heir apparent, the Prince of Wales. The Lancashire magistrates are nominated by this duchy officer, and not by the Lord Chancellor. The duchy is not confined to this county, but extends elsewhere, even to several parishes near Westbury-on-Severn, in Gloucestershire; Tutbury, etc. in Staffordshire; and the Savoy, in London, where the Dukes had a large palace.

The castle is the chief object of attraction. Standing on a hill, west of the town, on the site of one built after the Conquest, by Roger de Poitou, it includes the shire courts, county gaol, and other buildings, all in the castellated style, by Harrison (the architect of Chester Castle), and cost £140,000. Four or five old towers remain (in a restored condition), of which the dungeon (donjon), 90 feet high, is the oldest; and another, called Adrian's, which may have some Roman work in it. John of Gaunt's round tower, over the gate, is of the 14th century, as is also John of Gaunt's chair, another part of the building, from which, on a clear day may be distinctly seen the Isle of Man. Northcote's portrait of George III is in the Crown Court.

St Mary's, the parish church, stands on the same hill, and on the north of the Castle. The exterior walls of the church are of the date of the 15th century. It occupies the site of a Norman edifice built by Roger de Poitou, of which no vestige remains. The church is spacious and lofty, being 140 feet in length, 60 broad, and 40 high. It consists of a nave, two side aisles, and a chancel. Eight arches and pillars, of the old Anglo-Gothic, separate the nave from the side aisles, and extend nearly up to the altar. Recent alterations have materially changed the appearance of the church internally; plain glazed windows have given place to beautifully stained ones, the galleries have all been removed, and new ones erected at the west end.

From the churchyard, looking up the vale of the Lune, is seen first a viaduct of wood on the skew plan, which carries you over the branch line of 3 miles long to Poulton, on Morecambe Bay, a pretty watering-place, now much patronised by strangers.

Further up the Lune is an excellent five-arched bridge, which unites the town to the suburb of Skerton, and forms a bold and handsome entrance into the town from the north; and again further up the Lune is the Aqueduct Bridge, with five semi-circular arches, each with a 70 feet span, and 51 feet high. This magnificent undertaking conveys the Lancaster Canal over the Lune, and under one of the above arches the North Western Line passes up to Yorkshire.

The exterior of the church, with its lofty steeple, and the towers of the Castle, are noble objects for the stranger's eye as he passes onward by the Lancaster and Carlisle Line to the Lune Viaduct, which is in the immediate vicinity of the

Top left:
The Promenade, Morecambe. Once a major ferry port, with ships sailing to the Isle of Man, Barrow and Ireland, Morecambe's Stone Pier eventually became a shipbreaking site. It was all demolished and made way for the LMS's fabulous Deco Midland Hotel, which has now been restored. This view shows the promenade, with an LNWR advertising board behind the seated holidaymakers.

Middle: Like many seaside towns, Morecambe boasted its piers, such as the West Pier, shown here *c.* 1895.

Bottom: Lancaster was in a strategically important location. Its castle was built in the eleventh century and was one of Europe's longest operational prisons, until 2011. The Pendle witches were kept here, tried and executed in the castle too.

Castle Station. It crosses the Lune on three wide-span wood arches, extending to the north with a stone arch, over the Lancaster and Morecambe railway, and to the south with seven lofty stone arches across the road above the new wood landing-wharf; the buttress between each is perforated with two doorway arches. Owing to its great elevation above the river it forms a prominent object from many points of view in the vicinity of the Lancaster Castle Station, which is situated at the northern terminus of the Lancaster and Preston Railway; the station is a very neat building, erected of fine white freestone.

Professor Owen and Professor Whewell both are natives of Lancaster, and received their education at the Grammar School.

From the Lune Viaduct the line proceeds towards the shores of Morecambe Bay to

HEST BANK

Telegraph station at Lancaster, 3 miles.

This is a small and pretty village. A few families resort to it in summer for quiet and retirement, and in addition they have every combination of beautiful scenery with the wide expansive bay, surrounded by the Westmoreland and Cumberland mountains, and when the tide is out, a wide expanse of sands. There is a road across these sands at low water to the Furness side of the bay; a guide is stationed on them by Government, to accompany travellers across the channels, quicksands sometimes rendering crossing dangerous. The lover of scenery will be delighted with the magnificent and bold scenery which presents itself, as the train passes onwards along the shore of Morecambe to the Bolton-le-Sands station, and thence to

CARNFORTH

Population, 393.
A telegraph station.

Two miles distant is a limestone cave, 800 feet deep, called Dunal Mill Hole, out of which a stream issues underground, and falls into the sea near the village. In the vicinity is Carnforth Lodge, seat of T. Jackson, Esq.

The line then proceeds along an embankment of great length, and reaches the Burton and Holme station. The former, Burton-in-Kendal, is a market town, with a population of 751. It contains an ancient church with side chapels, with monument of Cockin. Six miles beyond is Kirkby Lonsdale, a market town, with a fine old Norman church, which commands a beautiful view of the Valley Lune and Ingleborough; antique old market cross, grammar school, old stone bridge across the river, and an old inn mentioned by 'Drunken Barnaby', and the latter is noted for its flax mills under Holme Fell and Tarleton Knot. When opposite Burton we pass from the county of Lancaster into

Above: It is possible just to glimpse parts of Kendal as the train hurtles through the undulating countryside towards Low Gill, which has one of the highest embankments in England.

Left: Sizergh Castle, 4 miles south of Kendal, is now owned by the National Trust.

Cumbria

WESTMORLAND

The name of which county is descriptive of its nature, that is the West-moor-land, a region of lofty mountains, naked hills, and bleak barren moors. The vallies through which the rivers flow are tolerably fertile; and in the north-eastern quarter there is a considerable tract of cultivated land. The south-western side is fertile, with a warmer climate. These two sides of the county are divided by lofty fells and extensive moors, intersected with pastoral vales. The climate is exceedingly humid, owing to its contiguity to the western ocean, from which the winds blow at least two-thirds of the year, and with them a quantity of moisture, which afterwards falls in the form of rain. The atmosphere is, however, pure and healthy. Fourteen miles from Lancaster the line crosses the river Bela, and thence passes on the east side of Milnthorpe, by Rowell, Lower Woodhouse, Greenhead, and east of Hincester.

BURTON Station.

MILNTHORPE

A telegraph station.
Hotel: Cross Keys.
Market Day: Friday.
Fairs: May 12th and Oct. 17th.

This place is a market town, with a population of 1,433, who are employed in the coasting trade, flax, flour, and paper mills. It contains a fine Gothic church, school, and chapel. In the vicinity are Dallam Tower, seat of George E. Wilson, Esq. Levens Hall, Hon. Mrs Howard. Sizergh Castle, the ancient seat of the Stricklands.

The line thence crosses the canal at the tunnel, and pursues its course through a fine and well-wooded country, to the pleasant village of Sedgwick. At this point the magnitude of the Sedgwick embankment is seen to advantage. The course of the line is now by Natland to Oxenholme, previous to which it crosses the Burton turnpike road, about 2 miles south of Kendal. After passing an embankment, and through some heavy rock cutting, the train reaches the Oxenholme station. At this point the line is joined by the Kendal and Windermere railway, which affords an easy and delightful means of access to the lake district from the north and south east.

A fine view of the town of Kendal is enjoyed at this station, the church spires, and blue roofs of the white houses which in the vale beneath; whilst far beyond rise the mountains of the west, the giants of the lake district.

Above: Oxenholme had a station and engine shed out of all proportion to the settlement it served. An Up mixed goods has just travelled through the station, in the distance to the right.

Below: Hauled by British Railways Standard Pacific No. 71000 *Duke of Gloucester*, the Up Glasgow–Birmingham passes the Lune Gorge near Tebay. 71000 is now preserved and based at Crewe, but in need of a major overhaul at present (2014).

Preston, Lancaster, & Carlisle Main Line continued

Oxenholme to Carlisle.

From Oxenholme the line proceeds upon embankments and through cuttings, with occasional views of Kendal and its venerable old castle. Soon after passing the Birkland cutting, the line skirts the base of the lofty Benson Knot, one of the highest hills in the neighbourhood, thence through heavy rock cuttings, and across an embankment, we arrive at Docker Gill viaduct, one of the most beautiful structures on the line. It consists of six arches stretching across a valley. Half a mile from this splendid viaduct, the line is carried past Morsedale Hag and half a mile farther northward we arrive at Grayrigg Summit, where the line passes through a heavy cutting of hard material called samel.

A mile onward is the Low Gill embankment, one of the highest in England.

LOW GILL AND SEDBERGH

Distance from station, 5 miles. A telegraph station.

Market Day at Sedbergh, on Wednesday.

Fairs at Sedbergh, March 20th, Whit-Wednesday, and October 29th.

Five miles distant is the market town of Sedbergh, on the Rothern, a beautiful romantic valley, surrounded by mountains. It has a population of 2,346, who are employed in the cotton mills, and Dr Lupton's Free Grammar School, founded in 1552, having three fellowships and ten scholarships at St John's College, Cambridge, attached thereto. In the vicinity is Ingniere Hall, on the Lune, seat of Mr Upton. Under Calf Fell is the beautiful waterfall, Cantley Spout, and near Borrow Bridge village is the Roman Camp, Castlehow.

The railway now skirts the Dillicar hills, and the scenery around increases in picturesque beauty and grandeur. At various points the windings of the silvery Lune are discerned from the line, and soon afterwards the train passes through the great Dillicar cut. The line is carried over the Borrow Water, near its junction with the Lune, upon a neat viaduct.

About twenty yards from the line stands the remains of the ancient Roman station of Castle Field, by which the mountain pass was anciently defended. The railway now passes Borrow Bridge, a romantic spot, celebrated for trout fishing, the scenery about which is the most beautiful along the whole line, and the traveller seems to be completely hemmed in on all sides by stupendous hills. The village of Borrow Bridge appears on the right, at a short distance from the line, and near it winds the beautiful stream of the Lune.

Passing through the Borrow Bridge cutting we reach the Lune embankment, 95 feet deep, formed through the old bed of the river, which has been diverted from its course, through a tunnel excavated in the

Left: Mardale church. In the 1930s, Hawes Water was dammed and, in 1935, the village of Mardale disappeared under the extended lake, which became a reservoir. Both the church and the famous Dun Bull Hotel disappeared. The church was dismantled and parts used in the reservoir's dam.

Below: Tebay locomotive shed, 14 March 1937.

Bottom: Shap Abbey was built in around 1199 and was closed in 1540. Some of its stone was used to build Lowther Castle.

solid rock, 50 feet from the top, and made nearly parallel to the ravine. Proceeding onwards we pass the Lune excavations, Loup's Fell cutting, the Birbeck embankment, and the Birbeck viaduct – thence we arrive at the foot of the great incline – a plain of 8 miles, rising 1 in 75, till it reaches the Shap summit.

TEBAY

A telegraph station.

Three miles to the north of Tebay station, close to Tebay Fell, lies the market town of Orton, under Orton Scar, the neighbourhood of which is rich in mineral treasures. The vicarage of All Saints was held by Burn of Orton Hall, author of the *Justice of Peace*. Remains of Castle Folds and other camps, tumuli, etc, are to be seen. Here is a market on Friday, and Fairs, May 3rd, Friday before Whit-Sunday, 2nd Friday after Michaelmas (for cattle). Close at hand is Langdale, of which place Bishop Barlow was a native. At Black Dub, on the Lyvennet, is an obelisk, in memory of Charles II having reviewed his troops on that spot on their return from Scotland in 1651. Proceeding from Tebay station we arrive at

SHAP WELLS

A telegraph station. Population, 991.
Market Day: Monday. Fair: May 4th.

Which has a saline spring, a Victoria pillar, close to the inn, an electric telegraph station, and contains remains of an abbey founded in 1119, by Thomas Gospatrick, who belonged to the Hogarth family, and tombs of the Vipouts, Cliffords, etc., who were buried here. The railway passes through the fells, over which the Pretender and his army marched in 1745. At Carl Lofts are Danish stones, a mile long, and at Gumerkeld there still remains a Druid circle. Mills the critic was a native of Hardendale, distant 1 mile. Five miles beyond is Hawes Water, and 8 miles to the east,

Appleby, the county town of Westmorland. The town is a very old one, having been associated with reminiscences not altogether of the most pleasing character from the time of the Norman Conquest.

A mile and a half farther we reach the Shap Summit, the highest point of the most stupendous work on the line. We are now 888 feet above the level of the line at Morecambe Bay, and 1,000 feet above the level of the sea. Rising 60 feet overhead, on each side are rugged walls of hard rock, presenting a truly magnificent appearance.

Leaving the Shap summit, we enter a cutting through limestone rock, and before it approaches Shap village, the line rims through a circle of large boulder stones, said to be the inner circle of an ancient Druidical temple.

From Shap the line proceeds on the east side of the town of Shap, along a heavy cutting, and passing thence under a skew bridge, along the flat

Left: An LNWR express to Aberdeen at Shap Summit *c.* 1903. There are a mix of both mail carriages and coaches being hauled.

Middle: The Lune Valley, with Shap Summit, has always been a favourite spot for photographers. This view of LMS No. 6113 was taken in the 1920s. Note the contrast in rolling stock from the above picture. Gone are the six-wheeled carriages to be replaced by vestibule coaches. At this time, many were still built of wood but soon carriages would be of all metal construction.

Below: Brougham Castle, near Penrith, *c.* 1890.

ABERDEEN EXPRESS ON SHAP SUMMIT.

portion of the route called Shap Mines, and following the valley of the stream, the line again runs under the turnpike road, and thence passes Thrimby, through a thick plantation.

Here the character of the scenery is considerably altered, the bare, rugged, and sterile mountains being succeeded by fertile pastures and picturesque prospects.

The Kendal turnpike road is crossed for the last time, by a skew bridge at Clifton, near the entrance to Lowther Park, 6,000 acres in extent, in which, hidden by a forest of huge trees, stands Lowther Castle, the noble Gothic seat of the Earl of Lonsdale, built by Smirke in 1808.

The scenery between Shap and Clifton is very attractive; Cross Fell, Saddleback, Skiddaw, and the other hills in the lake district appearing to great advantage.

CLIFTON
Population, 342. Telegraph station at Shap, 7½ miles.

In this neighbourhood, at Clifton Moor, a skirmish was fought in 1745, between the Pretender and the Duke of Cumberland, which is beautifully described by Sir Walter Scott, in *Waverley*. Here is a mineral well, and the old turreted ruin close to the farmhouse was the seat of the Wybergs. In the church there is some good stained glass.

From Clifton station we are carried along the Lowther embankment, and about 50 miles from Lancaster, and 20 from Carlisle, we cross the river Lowther on a magnificent viaduct, one of the most beautiful works of art on the line, 100 feet above the stream. Its arches, six in number, are of 60 feet span each. A mile and a half beyond, the line crosses the Eamont, on a viaduct of great beauty, consisting of five semi-circular arches. On the right is Brougham Hall, the seat of Lord Brougham, close to the old castle.

Leaving the county of Westmorland at this point we enter

CUMBERLAND

The two counties being divided by the stream which we have just crossed.

This county presents the traveller with, perhaps the grandest and most romantic scenery to be met with in England. The south western districts, particularly, form a gigantic combination of rugged, rocky mountains, thrown together with the wildest and rudest sublimity, yet enclosing the softest and most beautiful vallies, fairy streams, lakes, and rich and extensive woodlands, whilst, beside the charms given by nature to this favoured county, it boasts the picturesque and interesting addition of many baronial castles, Roman remains, and even Druidical monuments. Its surface is extremely irregular and broken. On the eastern confines of the county, a high range of hills stretches as far as Scotland, and at their feet a broad tract of land extends its whole length, partly cultivated, and partly heathy common. It is watered by the Eden and several other small streams. This tract becomes very extensive

Top: Devonshire Street, Penrith. The town is a major traffic centre, with the A66, M6 and A686 all meeting here. The railway station, now known as Penrith North Lakes, was opened in 1846. Penrith was also once a railway junction with lines going to the Lakes from the town.

Middle: Carlisle Citadel station is also the meeting point of numerous railway lines. It once saw the mix of liveries and locomotives associated with the Glasgow & South Western Railway, Caledonian, North British, Midland, London & North Western and North Eastern railways.

Below: A Caledonian 2-4-0, No. 52, at Carlisle in the 1890s. Note the lack of weather protection. The route up past Beattock could be terrible in winter and these cabs offered little comfort for driver or fireman.

before it reaches Carlisle, extending along the country to Wigton.

Proceeding on from the frontier, the line immediately enters a large cutting – and then running nearly level to the town of Penrith, we shortly after reach the station adjoining the ruins of the ancient castle.

PENRITH

Population, 7,189. A telegraph station. Hotel: New Crown.

Market Days: Tuesdays and Saturdays. Fairs: March 1st, April 5th and 24th, 3rd Tuesday in Oct., Whit and Martinmas Tuesday.

Penrith is a large market town. It contains race stand, assembly, news and library rooms, free grammar school, founded by Bishop Strickland, in 1340, girls school. St Andrew's church, rebuilt in 1722, contained a chantry, built by Bishop Strickland, who was the first to have water conveyed to this place. It contains an old tower, and portraits, in stained glass, of Richard Plantagenet and his wife. The grave of Gevain (the giant), 15 feet long, with two pillar crosses, 11½ feet high, and the giant's thumb, with a cross, 5¼ feet high, are in the churchyard. The walls of the castle still remain, and from the Beacon Hill an extensive view of unsurpassable beauty is obtained. In the vicinity are Ulleswater Lake and Eden, the latter the seat of Sir G. Musgrave, Bart., rebuilt in 1852, 'at which is an old drinking glass, called the "Luck of Eden Hall," a gift of the fairies, the breaking of which, it is said, will bring misfortune to the house.' *Sharp's British Gazetteer.*

From Penrith the country is flat and uninteresting. The line enters the valley of the Petteril, through which it pursues almost a direct course to Carlisle, past the following stations, viz: Plumpton, Calthwaite, Southwaite, and Wreay. In the vicinity are Hutton Hall, Sir R. Vane, Bart.; Barrock Fell, Newbiggin Hail; and Petterill Bank, J. Fawcett, Esq.

CARLISLE

A telegraph station. Hotels: County; Bush; Crown and Mitre; White Hart.

Market Days: Wednesdays and Saturdays.

Fairs: August 26th, Sept. 19th, every Saturday from Michaelmas to Christmas, on the Sands, Saturday at Whitsuntide and Martinmas. Races in July.

A cathedral town, parliamentary borough, and port, with a population of about 29,417, who return two members, in a healthy spot on the Eden, in Cumberland, near the Scottish border. Formerly it was the key to Scotland on this side of the island. The Romans made it one of their chief stations on Hadrian's wall, by the name of Luguvallium; and here the famous Briton, King Arthur, held his court. Cottons, ginghams, chintzes, checks, and hats are made in considerable quantities. One factory (Dixon's) is marked by an eight-sided brick chimney 305 feet high. A railway, 10 miles long, reaches (where the wall ended) to Bowness on the Solway Firth.

It is also celebrated for its manufacture of fancy biscuits, which are produced in a most complete state, all by machinery, and to an extent that would certainly astonish visitors. The leading establishment in this branch of trade is that of Messrs Carr & Co.; and if curiosity should induce the tourist to make a visit to the manufactory of this noted firm, we do not hesitate to say that it would be found highly interesting. If any prejudice exist against the free use of fancy biscuits, it will at once be removed, on an inspection of the works and the process of production, even from the minds of the most fastidious; the most scrupulous cleanliness being observable throughout the whole works.

The Cathedral which has lately been restored and much embellished, under the superintendence of Owen Jones, and rendered more imposing by the removal of a block of buildings, which hid it, to some extent, from the passer by, was originally part of a Norman priory, and is cruciform, though a portion of the nave is gone; the other part is turned into a parish church. Length, 242 feet; tower, 130 feet high. The beautiful east window is 48 feet high. There are two or three fine brasses, and a monument to Paley. Near it are the Deanery, and a refectory, now used as the Chapter-house, the original one having been pulled down in the civil wars. The restored Castle includes William Rufus' Keep and the barracks. Henry I made it a bishop's see.

Some of the oldest houses are in the market place, whence several well built streets diverge. Here stands a cross, built in 1682, and the ancient Moot-hall. The Court House and County Gaol is an extensive pile by Smirke, at a cost of £100,000, who also built the new bridge over the Eden – an excellent stoneway, on five arches of 65 feet span each, which cost £70,000. There are two others across the Caldew. The Library and News Room is a work of Rickman's. There is a County Hospital, with a Grammar School, founded by Henry VIII, at which Bishop Thomas and Dean Carlyle, a native, were scholars. At the Dispensary, in 1788, 'a child was born without any brain, and lived six days.' The Pretender's son, Charles Stuart, was here in 1745, on his march to the south. The reader will not forget Fergus MacIvor's death in *Waverley*. In 1786 shocks of an earthquake were felt here.

Several interesting spots are in this quarter. The Roman (or Picts') Wall may be traced at various points, near the railway to Newcastle. Rickerby, seat of G. H. Head, Esq. Corby Castle, seat of P. H Howard, Esq., has the claymore of MacIvor (whose real name was Macdonald). Up the Irthing, down the moors, is Naworth Castle, belonging to the Earl of Carlisle (a Howard), better known as Lord Morpeth, brother to the Duchess of Sutherland. Formerly it was the seat of Belted Will (Lord Will Howard), when guardian of the marches in Elizabeth's reign. A poor kind of coal is dug here. From the Moot Hill, near Brampton, there is a splendid view of the Cheviots. Rose Castle, the Gothic seat of the Bishop of Carlisle, lies situated in a fine well-wooded part of the Caldew.

Left: Carlisle, just over the border, was a busy railway centre where the lines of seven companies (three Scottish, four English) met. Having travelled north from Shap, the fall into Carlisle gave a rest before the steep inclines and summit at Beattock.

Above and left: Gretna Green was once the favoured choice of runaway grooms and brides. Above is Gretna from the station, and left is Carter's store in this little village, both *c.* 1910.

Scotland

Carlisle to Edinburgh and Glasgow

CARLISLE

The railway station in Court Square was built from a design by Mr Tite, the architect of the London Royal Exchange, and of all the station houses on this line.

Upon starting from the station, the traveller will observe on his right hand the outer wall of the Castle, above that the front of the Deanery, and further over, the ancient towers of the Cathedral. On the left the canal to the Solway, and Dixon's factory. Proceeding onwards, we cross the Calder over a viaduct, and thence over the river Eden by another viaduct, after which the line proceeds through King Moor, and arrives at the Rockcliffe station. Leaving Rockcliffe, in a few minutes we arrive at the river Esk, which gives its name to Eskdale, one of the most beautiful places in Scotland. On the banks of the river, not visible, however, from the railway, is situated the 1st Sir James Graham's elegant mansion of Netherby.

Crossing the river on a seven-arched viaduct, we have a fine view to the north-west; thence passing over the Glasgow road, we can perceive the Solway on the right, and Langholm Hills, with Sir John Malcolm's monument on the left. We now proceed along the Guard's embankment, formed through a deep moss, which absorbed thousands of tons of earth before the foundation was sufficiently solid to bear a train. Shortly after this we reach the FLORISTON station. We then cross the Sark, and leaving the county of Cumberland, enter Dumfriesshire, one of the most important of the southern counties of Scotland.

The next station is now in view, and soon recognised as the celebrated

GRETNA

Telegraph station at Carlisle, 9 miles. Hotel: Gretna Hall.

Post Horses, Flys, etc., at the station and hotel. Tariff – 1s 6d per mile; post boy, 3d per mile; one horse vehicle, 1s per mile or 15s per day; gig, 12s per day; riding horse, 6s to 7s per day; pony, 5s to 5s 6d per day.

Money Order Office at Carlisle.

The village of Gretna Green, in Dumfries, Scotland, is built on the banks of the Solway Firth, 8 miles north of Carlisle. It is the first stage in Scotland from England, and has for more than eighty years been known as the place for the celebration of the marriages of fugitive lovers from England. According

Top left: Thomas Carlyle was still alive and writing when *Bradshaw's Guide* was published. His house in Ecclefechan is now a tourist attraction.

BRUCE'S STATUE, LOCHMABEN.

Left: 'Lochmaben is well worthy of a visit', not least for the statue of Robert the Bruce outside the town hall.

to the Scottish law, it was only necessary for a couple to declare before a justice of the peace that they were unmarried, and wished to be married, in order to render the ceremony lawful. An Act of Parliament has since come into operation which requires a residence in Scotland of too long a duration to suit the purpose of fugitive lovers, and the blacksmith of Gretna Green, like Othello, will now find his 'occupation gone'. More than 300 marriages took place annually in this and the neighbouring village of Springfield, and the fees varied from one to forty guineas.

Proceeding onward, the line passes the junction of the Dumfries line and Gretna Hall, through Graham's Hill cutting, and opens into a fine view, which about this point presents a most picturesque, varied, and highly romantic appearance.

Upon leaving Kirkpatrick station the line soon crosses the 'gently winding Kirtle', on a viaduct of nine arches, and then passes the tower of Robert Gill, a noted freebooter, who, with many other reckless 'chields' of former times, made this district the scene of their border raids.

Shortly after leaving Kirtle Bridge station we pass through an extensive cutting, and thence over an embankment. We then cross the Mein Water and West Gill Burn, and soon arrive at

ECCLEFECHAN
Telegraph station at Lockerbie, 5½ miles. Hotel: Bush.
Market Day: Saturday (large pork market). Fairs: Once a month.

The town of Ecclefechan is remarkable for nothing but its frequent and well-attended markets and fairs. From the station may be perceived a strong square keep or tower, the seat of General Matthew Sharpe, and known as Hoddam Castle, formerly a place of considerable importance as a border stronghold, and at present distinguished as one of the most delightful residences in Dumfriesshire. Opposite the castle, on a conspicuous mount, stands Trailtron, known as the Tower of Repentance, and formerly used as a beacon. It is said that Sir Richard Steele, while residing near this place, saw a shepherd boy reading his Bible, and asked him what he learned from it. 'The way to heaven', answered the boy. 'And can you show it to me?' said Sir Richard, in banter. 'You must go by that tower,' replied the shepherd, and he pointed to the Tower of Repentance.

Leaving Ecclefechan, we obtain a grand and extensive view of the surrounding scenery, perhaps the most gorgeous on the whole line. The Solway at the base of its gigantic sentinel; and beyond, the lofty Skiddaw, with its top melting away in the clouds. And before us is Borren's Hill, which from its curious shape is conspicuous long before we come near it. Skirting Brakenhill, we next arrive at the Milk Water, another of the poetical streams of bonnie Scotland, crossed by a viaduct, which commands a prospect of surpassing beauty.

Left: The last stone of a 'Druid's Temple' at Lochmaben. The stone itself is 118 cubic feet and weighs some 20 tons in weight. Scotland abounds with standing stones, crannogs, brochs and other archaeological sites.

Below: These two images of Beattock show the difference in steam engine technology in fifty years. Above is the now-preserved *Princess Elizabeth* of the LMS Princess class of 1933 in British Railways livery. The lower image is a Caledonian Railway 4-4-0 locomotive of the 1880s.

LOCKERBIE

A telegraph station. Hotel: George.

Market Day: Thursday.

Fairs: Second Thursday in January, February, March, April, May, June, August, September, October, November, and before Christmas and Old Martinmas.

Bankers: Branch of Edinburgh & Glasgow Bank.

Lochmaben, in the vicinity, is well worthy of a visit. It is poetically called the 'Queen of the Lochs', from its situation amid so many sheets of water. Looking north from this station, there being no curve, we can see down the line a very long way. Here 'Old Mortality' died at Brick Hall, in 1801. Lockerbie Hall, J. Douglas, Esq., and Mains Tower, which belonged to the Johnstones, are close at hand.

From Nethercleugh station to the next there is scarcely an object of interest worth noticing. We pass Dinwoodie, Greens, and Mains, and then arrive at Wamphray. Behind Raehill, a fine mansion situated on the banks of the Kinnel, towers the hill of Queensberry, one of the highest mountains in the south of Scotland. Shortly after leaving the Wamphray station, we cross the Annan, on a structure 350 feet in length. Farther on, a long embankment, succeeded by the Logrie cutting. Advancing, we cross once more the Glasgow road, and in a few minutes reach the place where all the visitors to Moffat will alight, at

BEATTOCK (Moffat)

A telegraph station. Hotel: Beattock. Market Day: Saturday.

Fairs: Third Friday in March, July 29th, Oct. 15th and 20th.

Money Order Office. Bankers: Branch of Union Bank of Scotland.

About 2 miles from Beattock, surrounded on every side but one by lofty hills, lies the fashionable village of

Moffat, celebrated for its mineral waters. The environs are remarkably beautiful, and the different villas exceedingly pretty. Moffat has long been farmed for its mineral waters (the sulphur Spa discovered in 1639, and the iron springs at Hartfell, in 1780), and visitors will find every accommodation, including Assembly Rooms, Baths, etc. Among the fine scenery scattered round Moffat, are Bell Craig, and the Grey Mare's Tail waterfall, the latter being one of the grandest sights it is possible to conceive. The water is precipitated over a rock 300 feet high. In the vicinity are Raehills, Earl Hopetoun; Drumcrieff, formerly Dr Currie's seat. The Mole Hill, with its camps, and Bell Craig, which commands an extensive view, and where delicious whey milk can be procured.

Resuming our progress from the Beattock station, we proceed onwards through the lovely vale of Annandale, and then passing a deep cutting, we skirt the Greskin Hills, close to which are the sources of three of Scotland's

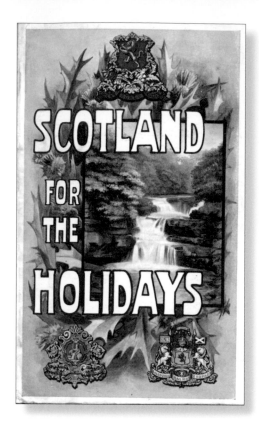

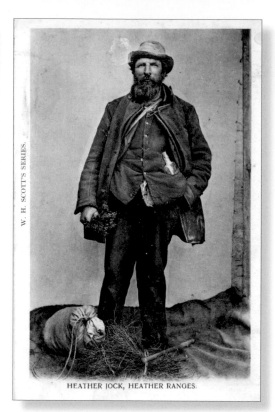

W. H. SCOTT'S SERIES.

HEATHER JOCK, HEATHER RANGES.

Above, left: West Coast Route brochure from *c.* 1910. The railway which operated the routes to Scotland marketed themselves from an early age as East Coast and West Coast routes.

Above, right: Heather Jock, an Abington worthy.

Below: Elvanfoot was the junction for the Leadhills & Wanlockhead Light Railway, which took the passenger to the highest villages in Scotland.

finest rivers; the Tweed, the Clyde, and the Annan having their rise in the same clump of hills, and each falling into a different sea, in a different part of the kingdom.

The great viaduct over the Elvan is well worth attention. Passing Elvanfoot station, where the Clyde and Elvan Water join, we reach

ABINGTON

A telegraph station at Symington, 9 miles. Hotel: Hunter's.
Money Order Office at Biggar, 14 miles.

We now begin to perceive a distinct stream of the Clyde, which shortly after issuing from its source, from the accession of many tributary burns, becomes at this point, a river of considerable size, and keeps gradually increasing:

Now sunk in shades, now bright in open day,
Bright Clyde, in simple beauty, wends his way.

This is the junction of the Clyde and Glengowner water. Some gold was found here in the time of James VI.

Previous to arriving at the next station, we pass, on the right hand, Lamington Old Tower, one of the seats of the family, one of whose daughters, it is said, was married to the great Hero of Scotland, Sir William Wallace.

Passing Lamington Station, close to which are hilly sheep walks, porphyry, and good trout fishing, Lamington House, Wandell Bower, Windgate House, Arbery Hill (600 feet high), Whitchill (70 yards), Hartside, Woodend, and Braehead, with their Roman and Saxon camps, Druid arches, and Cauldchapel, with its moat of 20 yards, we arrive at

SYMINGTON

A telegraph station.

A short time previous to reaching the station, we have the famous hill of Tinto appearing in view; towering high above the other giants of nature which surround it. Visitors ascend to the top of Tinto or the 'Hill of Fire,' in order to enjoy the fine view from its summit. In the vicinity are Fatlips Castle, in ruins, and Castle Hill, which is planted all over.

SYMINGTON, BIGGAR, AND BROUGHTON

This is a line, 19½ miles long, running out of the Caledonian, at Symington, to Peebles, 8¼ miles of which only are yet open. The line passes, via the station of Coulter to Biggar – A small town situated in a hilly district, with a population of about 1,550. The church, built by the Flemings, is in the form of a cross. Traces of a Roman camp may also be seen.

Clockwise from top left:

Carstairs station was the junction for the line to Edinburgh.

The village itself was populated by people who worked on the railway.

Midcalder was a mile distant from the station that served the town.

Auchengrey Junction signal box.

Carnwath village.

Broughton, in the vicinity of which are some border castle ruins. This forms the present terminus of the line.

Caledonian Main Line continued

Thankerton and the neighbouring village of Corington Mill are celebrated as having been a favourite haunt of the persecuted Covenanters, and there are many spots pointed out among the surrounding hills as their places of worship. The Clyde, in the vicinity, is remarkable for its many windings.

Leaving Thankerton, and once more crossing the river, we shortly reach the Carstairs Junction, from which point the line forks; the right branch turning off to Edinburgh and the left to Glasgow.

Carstairs to Edinburgh

CARSTAIRS JUNCTION

Population, about 1,066. A telegraph station.

Money Order Office, Lanark, 5¼ miles.

Here are remains of the Bishops of Glasgow's castle, castle dykes, Roman camp of upwards of five acres, and Carstairs House, which is the seat of R. Monteith, Esq.

Carnwath – Here are remains of Couthalley Castle, Carnwath House, the beautiful seat of the Somervilles, and the church, which contains their effigies and tombs. Here is also the kennel of the Linlithgow hounds.

Auchengrey and Harburn stations, close to which is Harburn House, the seat of J. Young, Esq.

MIDCALDER

Population, about 1,474. Distance from station, 1 mile. Telegraph station at Carstairs, 7½ miles. Hotel: Lemon Tree. Bankers: Edinburgh and Glasgow Bank.

Close at hand is Calder House, seat of Lord Torpichen, in which is a fine portrait of Knox, who first administered the sacrament here after the Reformation. Greenbank was the native place of Archbishop Spottiswoode, the church historian.

Currie – The scene of Ramsay's *Gentle Shepherd*, and near which is Currie Hill, the seat of the Skenes, and close by the ruins of Lennox Tower, the residence of Queen Mary and Darnley; Buberton, the hunting seat of James VI, and for some time the abode of Charles X of France, after the events of 1830.

Kingsknowe and Slateford stations, at the latter of which fairs are held on the Wednesday after the 26th August and the Friday before Kirriemuir fair.

NEW LANARK

Above: New Lanark was the site of David Dale's cotton mill, now a World Heritage Site.

The Lake Pavilion, Lanark.

Right: Lanark Loch.

Below: Another revolutionary form of transport came to Lanark in 1910, when a huge aviation meeting was held at the Racecourse.

J. A. DREXEL

AVIATION GROUND. LANARK. TINTO in distance.

Carstairs to Glasgow

Proceeding on to Glasgow the line passes Carstairs House, the seat of R. Monteith, Esq.

From Carstairs station we cross the river Mouse, which runs through some wild and romantic scenery, arriving at

Cleghorn, the junction of the branch to Lanark. Here are the ruins of an old chapel and a Roman camp.

Lanark Branch

Proceeding onwards, a distance of 2¾ miles, the whole of the neighbouring grounds to Lanark are remarkable as having been the hiding place of Sir William Wallace.

> Each ruggen rock proclaims great Wallace' fame,
> Each cavern wild is honour'd with his name,
> Here in repose was stretched his mighty form,
> And there he sheltered from the night and storm.

LANARK

Telegraph station at Carstairs, 5½ miles. Hotel: Clydesdale.

Market Days: Tuesday and Saturday.

Fairs: Last Tuesday in February, second Wednesday in April, last Wednesday in May and July, first Tuesday in July, first Wednesday in November, and last Tuesday in December.

Bankers: Commercial Bank of Scotland; City of Glasgow; the Royal.

From this point travellers can visit the Falls of Clyde, and the romantic scenery in the neighbourhood. Independent of the more than magnificent grandeur of the various waterfalls themselves, the beauty of the country on every side of the river, and the picturesque succession of views which present themselves to the eye at every turn of the road, are a source of great attraction. A guide to the Falls may be obtained at any of the respectable inns in the town.

The ancient town of Lanark, capital of the county, which returns one member, has a population of about 5,395, and although not engaging in outward appearance, possesses many points of interest, and it remarkable as having been the scene of Wallace's first grand military exploit, in which he killed Hoslerig, the English sheriff, and drove his soldiers from the town. The burgh consists of a principal street, and a number of smaller ones branching off. The grammar school had General Roy and Judge Macqueen as scholars. The church, built in 1774, contains a figure of Wallace. In the vicinity are Castle Hill tower, Quair Castle, Cleghorn, with its Roman camp, 600 yards by 420; Lee House, seat of Sir N. Lockhart, Bart., at which is the

Station Road, Carluke.

Top: Some 1,700 men, women and children were employed at New Lanark.

Above left: Station Road, Carluke.

Above right: Milton Lockhart, Carluke. This house is now in Japan, having been removed there stone by stone.

Left: A private loco of Wm Baird & Co. at Gartsherrie Works. The iron founders could operate their locos on the main lines.

'Lee Penny or Talisman.' Judge Lee, and Lithgow, the traveller, were born here.

New Lanark village is situated about one mile from Lanark, and contains a population of 1,807. It was established in 1784, by Robert Owen's father-in-law, the late David Dale, and is now the property of Messrs Walker & Co. There are several cotton mills, at which about 1,100 hands are employed. No stranger ought to omit visiting this far-famed village, which is quite in his way when visiting the Upper Falls of the Clyde.

The Falls: Bonnington Fall, athough the most inconsiderable, should be first visited, for the remarkable scenery surrounding it.

Curra Linn Fall, 84 feet, considered by some as the finest of the Falls, about half a mile from Bonnington, the seat of Sir Charles Ross, at which are Wallace's chair, cup, and portrait, is composed of three slight falls, at an inconsiderable distance from each other, over which the vast body of water rushes with fearful impetuosity into a deep abyss. To describe the beauties of the scene is an almost impossible task, requiring the glowing language of the poet to do justice to them.

Stonebyres. The approach to this (which is 70 feet) fall is by a gently winding road – its tout ensemble and the adjacent landscape is sublime. Above we have lofty crags fringed with natural wood. The torrent dashes in one uninterrupted stream into the abyss beneath, raising clouds of stormy spray from the boiling gulf.

Cartland Crags – which extends nearly half a mile on both sides of the river, is a most romantic dell, composed of lofty rocks, beautifully diversified with natural wood. The approach from the north – a level piece of ground, around which the Mouse makes a sweep – conducts to the mouth of this great chasm. As you enter, and through its whole extent, a succession of the most picturesque scenes appear on every hand. In the most sequestered part of the dell is a natural chasm in the rock, called Wallace's Cave, which tradition and history concur in informing us was often resorted to by that hero.

Upon emerging from Cartland Crags upon the south, the traveller finds himself surrounded by a beautiful amphitheatre of high grounds, open towards the Clyde, and in the immediate vicinity of the Bridge of Lanark.

Caledonian Main Line continued

Leaving Cleghorn and Braidwood stations (near the latter of which are extensive collieries and lime works), we arrive at

CARLUKE

Population, about 2,845. Distance from station, ½ mile.

Hotel: Commercial. Coach to Lanark and the Falls of the Clyde.

The line now passes through a district of country rich in mineral wealth – beautiful scenery – celebrated far and near as the Orchard of Scotland, and famous for its fine fruit. The growers clear very large sums by sending the produce of their orchard to Glasgow. On the left side of the railway, shortly after leaving the station, is Milton, a handsome building, in the Tudor style of architecture, situated on a fine peninsula, and skirted on three sides by the Clyde. Next appears the stately seat of Mauldslie Castle, belonging to the Hyndfords, and St Oswold's chapel, a hermitage. The next station is

OVERTOWN

Telegraph station at Motherwell, 4 miles.

All the scenery around is so enchanting that the traveller will wish the train to linger over it. Not far from this station is another beautiful spot called Cambusnethan, which attracts the notice and admiration of every stranger.

Passing Wishaw station, near which is Wishaw Castle, the seat of J. Hamilton, Esq. we reach

MOTHERWELL

A telegraph station. Money Order Office at Wishaw, 2½ miles.

From this junction we pass the stations of Holytown and Whifflet to

Coatbridge – At this place the Dundyvan Iron Works are well worth visiting.

Gartsherrie Junction – Proceeding a few miles beyond this station, we enter Stirlingshire.

Caledonian Main Line continued

Pursuing our course from the Motherwell station, we pass several places of note. The beautiful village of Uddingston is situated on an elevated spot, commanding an extensive and highly diversified prospect. The Clyde – the city of Glasgow, the Queen of the West – the numerous seats scattered around, the distant hills of Stirling, Dumbarton, and Argyllshires, lie extended before the eye, forming a panorama of great beauty. Then Newton station, and crossing the Clyde, we pass near

Cambuslang – Loudon the naturalist was a native, and in the vicinity are Kirkburn, with the remains of a chapel and hospital; Westburne. T. Hamilton, Esq., and here 'Cambuslang Wark' took place in 1742, at which Whitfield was an eye witness. This station forms the junction of the ...

Strathaven Branch

The only intermediate station between Cambuslang and Hamilton is 4 miles from the junction, which requires a very short space of time to annihilate.

BLANTYRE

In his visit, the stranger must not omit to see Blantyre Priory, Bothwell Bridge, where the Covenanters were defeated in 1679, by the Duke of Monmouth, and Chatelherault, a summer chateau of the Duke of Hamilton.

HAMILTON

A telegraph station. Hotels: Commercial; Bruce's Arms.

Market Day: Friday. Fairs: Last Tuesday in Jan., second Tuesday in Feb., Friday after 15th May, last Thursday in June, second Thursday in July and Nov.

Bankers: Branch of Commercial Bank of Scotland; Branch of British Linen Co.

Over the whole neighbourhood of this place lie scattered scenes full of historical and poetical interest; and the traveller making of it his headquarters, might in a short time see a 'whole Switzerland of romantic dells and dingles.' Many of the places here are classic ground, the interest never flagging, from its being immortalised by the pen of Sir Walter Scott, and other writers of lesser note.

Hamilton Palace, partly as old as 1591, the seat of the Duke of Hamilton, is a noble building. The grounds and picture gallery, in which is Ruben's 'Daniel in the Lions' Den,' are thrown open to strangers, without any formal application. Cullen was a native of Hamilton. The traveller must of course visit the ruins of Bothwell Castle, one of the most picturesque and venerable monuments of the ancient splendour of Scotland. Its stately grandeur excites the admiration of all who have seen it.

From hence the railway passes the stations of High Blantyre, Meikle Earnock, Quarter Road, and Glassford, to

Strathaven, supported principally by weaving and noted for the quality of its horses.

Caledonian Main Line continued

We have scarcely got clear of the junction at Cambuslang than the arrival of the train is announced at the ancient royal burgh of

RUTHERGLEN

Telegraph station at Glasgow, 2½ miles.

Here fairs are held on the first Friday after March 11th, 25th July, 25th August, May 4th, first Tuesday after June 4th, first Wednesday before first Friday in November, and first Friday after 25th December.

Above, left: Strathaven station in the 1950s.

Above, right: Hamilton Central Station.

Left: Stonefield, Blantyre.

Above, left: Rutherglen on a fair day sometime around 1904. Traffic problems were just as bad then as today, albeit with different reasons for the congestion. This is likely to be St Luke's Fair, which was held in October each year.

Above, right: Rutherglen was the site of the 1297 treaty between England and Scotland that was supposed to bring peace between the two nations. The treaty was either signed in the kirkyard shown here, or in the church itself to the left. The tower dates from the fifteenth century, but the gable of the old church can clearly be seen. Rutherglen has been a place of worship since at least the sixth century.

Rutherglen Church is famous on account of two great national transactions; it was here that Edward I signed the treaty in 1297, and Monteith covenanted to betray Wallace.

GLASGOW

Telegraph stations at the Exchange, and 147, Queen Street.

Hotels: Carrick's Royal Hotel; Walker's George Hotel; Bush's Buck's Head; McGregor's Queen Hotel. Restauranteurs: Ferguson and Forrester, 33, Buchanan Street; the Queen's, 81, Queen Street. News Rooms: Royal Exchange, Queen Street, and the Tontine, (free); Athenaeum, Ingram Street, and the Telegraphic, 27, Glassford Street, one penny per visit.

Coach Offices: J. Walker, 104, West Nile Street; Wylie and Lochhead, 28, Argyle Street; A. Menzies, 10, Argyle Street.

Steamers to and from Ardrishaig, 5½ hours, Helensburgh, in 2½ hours, Roseneath, 2½ hours, Gareloch Head, 4 hours, Gourock and Ashton, 2 hours, Inverkip, 3 hours, Wemyss Bay, 3¼ hours, Largs, 3½ hours, Millport, 3¾ hours, Kilmun, 3 hours, Dunoon, 3 hours, Inellan, 3½ hours, Rothesay, 3½ hours, Strone 2¾ hours, Crinan, 7½ hours, Oban, 2¾ hours, Inveraray, 7¼ hours, Arroquhar, 4½ hours, Lochgoilhead, 5 hours, &c.

Market Day: Wednesday. Fairs: May 26, second Monday in July.

Bankers: Branch Bank of Scotland; Branch of British Linen Co.; Branch Commercial Bank of Scotland; Branch National Bank of Scotland; Branch Royal Bank of Scotland; City of Glasgow Bank; Union Bank of London; Clydesdale Banking Co.; Union Bank of Scotland; North British Bank; Branch of Edinburgh & Glasgow Bank.

Glasgow: The first port and seat of manufacture in Scotland and a parliamentary burgh, two members, in the lower ward or division of Lanarkshire (which county also returns one member), on the Clyde, 50 miles from the open sea. That which was the ruin of many small places in this part of Great Britain, namely the Union, 1707, was the grand cause of the prosperity of Glasgow, which from its admirable position on a fine navigable river in the heart of a coalfield, and from the spirit of the inhabitants, has risen to be reckoned as the fourth port of the United Kingdom, and a rival to Manchester. When Bailie Nichol Jarvie and his worthy father, the deacon, 'praise to his memory,' lived in the Salt Market, before the American Revolution, it was a great place for the tobacco trade, but since 1792 cotton has been the staple business.

Population about 329,097, of which perhaps 50,000 are employed in the spinning, weaving, bleaching, and dyeing of cotton goods, worsted, muslin, silks, etc., while a large number are engaged in the manufacture of iron, brass, steam engines, glass, nails, pottery, umbrellas, hats, chemicals, and other branches of trade, and in wooden and iron ship building, besides numbers engaged in maritime and commercial transactions. These are

Top left: A Caledonian Railway 4-6-0 leaves Central Station.

Left: Locomotives under construction in Hyde Park Works, Glasgow. From here they would be brought to the river and exported worldwide.

Below: Glasgow Bridge, *c.* 1895.

the distinguishing characteristics of modern Glasgow, and the commercial activity and restlessness of its inhabitants have caused the immense impulse its trade has received within the last fifty years. The site is a level, 4 or 5 miles square, chiefly on the north side of the river. On the south side are the suburbs of Tradeston, Laurieston, and Hutchesonton; here are most of the factories. Its port is the open river, fronting the Broomielaw, lined by noble quays above 1 mile long, and so much deepened that first-class ships, which used to stop at Port Glasgow, 18 miles lower down, can now come up to the city. Formerly people could cross without wet feet, where now there is 20 feet of water. The tonnage owned by the port exceeds 150,000, its income is £90,000, and the customs (which in 1812 were only £3,100) amount to £700,000.

Bridges: Six cross the Clyde, in some parts 400 feet wide. Jamaica Bridge, near the Ayr railway and Broomielaw, rebuilt by Telford in 1833, 500 feet long, 60 wide. A wooden bridge rebuilt in 1853, Victoria Bridge, rebuilt in 1851–53 by Walker, on five granite arches, the middle one being 80 feet span, and the next two 76 feet. It replaces old Stockwell Bridge, which was begun in 1345. Hutcheson Bridge built in 1833, by R. Stevenson, the builder of the wooden bridge, opened 1855. Rutherglen Bridge is the highest, near the King's Park, in which stands the Nelson pillar.

City and Commercial Buildings: The large new County Buildings are in Wilson-street. Justiciary or Law Courts, in the Salt Market, near Hutcheson Bridge, has a Grecian portico, imitated from the Parthenon. County Bridewell, Duke Street, an excellent self-supporting institution, built in 1824, in the Norman style. Large City Hall, in the Candleriggs-street, built in 1840. Old Town Hall in the Trongate – in front is Flaxman's statue of William IV. Exchange in Queen Street, a handsome Grecian building by D. Hamilton, erected in 1840, 200 ft long by 76 broad; fine Corinthian eight-column portico and tower; news-room, 130 feet long. In front is Baron Marchetti's bronze statue of Wellington. Hamilton is also the architect of the Theatre Royal, in Dunlop Street, and the City of Glasgow bank, the latter copied from the temple of Jupiter Stater. Union Bank and the handsome Assembly Room, now the Athenaeum, in Ingram street. Corn Exchange, in the Italian style, built in 1842. Trades' Hall, a domed building. Western Club House, in Buchanan street. Cleland Testimonial, in Sauchihall street, raised to commemorate the services of Dr Cleland to the city. Post Office, in George Square. Campell's warehouse in Candleriggs and Ingram streets. The Vulcan Foundry, belonging to Mr Napier, who established the steamers between this, Greenock, and Belfast in 1818, where iron steam-ships and engines for the great mail steamers are built. St Rollox's Chemical Works, north of the town, having an enormous chimney 440 feet high. Monteith's large cotton and bandana factory at Barrowfield.

Churches: There are above 120 churches and chapels, the most conspicuous of which is St Mungo's High Church, on a hill at the top of High-Street. It

JAMAICA BRIDGE, GLASGOW, AND S.S. CARRICK, R.N.V.R. CLUB. (SCOTLAND.) B.4235.

Top left: Glasgow Bridge, being at the end of Jamaica Street, is also known as Jamaica Bridge. For a long time, the SV *Carrick* was berthed as a club for the Royal Naval Volunteer Reserve in Glasgow. Originally the clipper *City of Adelaide*, she sank at her moorings and was salvaged and 'parked' at Irvine, where she deteriorated and was so nearly scrapped. In 2014, she set sail for Australia and a full resoration, exactly 150 years after she entered service.

BROOMIELAW, GLASGOW.

Left: The Broomielaw, where steamers left for the Clyde Coast and Western Isles, with three pleasure steamers full of holidaymakers. The ships are the *Eagle III*, *Isle of Bute* and the *Benmore*.

Below: Glasgow Necropolis in 1905. The graveyard had opened in 1833, soon after the Cemeteries Act had been passed, and contains the final resting places for many of the great and the good of the Second City of the Empire. Alexander 'Greek' Thomson designed numerous of the tombs as did Charles Rennie Mackintosh. The Blackie publishing family tomb was designed by Talwin Morris.

was part of a monastery planted here by St Mungo (or Kentigern) in the 6th century, when the town was first founded, and was an Archbishop's Cathedral till episcopacy was abolished by the General Assembly which met here in 1638, in the Mace Church. It is a venerable stone building without transepts, 300 feet long, having a tower 224 feet high, and an ancient crypt of the 12th century, full of monuments, and once used as a church (see Rob Roy). There are about 150 pillars and as many windows. Close to it is the Barony Church. A short bridge crosses the ravine (here 250 feet deep) of Molendinar Burn to the Necropolis, where a monument to Knox was placed in 1845. St John's Church was Dr Chalmers's, many of whose labours and writings were commenced here. The College Church is as old as 1699; Tron Church tower as old as 1484; St Andrew's has a good portico; St George's, a spire of 160 feet; St Enoch's was built by Hamilton. Near the Custom House is the Gothic Roman Catholic Chapel. In George's Square are – Sir Walter Scott's monument, Chantrey's statue of Watt, the inventor of the modern steam engine, and Flaxman's of Sir J. Moore, the last of whom was born at Glasgow in 1761.

University, Schools, etc.: The University, in High Street, visited by Queen Victoria in 1849, one of the oldest buildings in the city, was founded in 1453, by Bishop Turnbull, and consists of two or three brick courts, in the French style, with a good staircase at the entrance; at some distance behind is Dr Hunter's Museum, in the Grecian style, containing objects of anatomy, natural history, books, autographs, illuminations, and Chantrey's bust of Watt, who was at first mathematical instrument maker to the University. The most curious thing is a Paisley shirt, woven without a seam or joining. The College Library includes about 80,000 volumes. The senior students, called togati, dress in scarlet gowns, and the whole number of 1,200 is divided into nations, according to the district they come from. Beyond the Museum is Macfarlan's Observatory.

Andersonian University, in the old Grammar School, George Street, is a place for gratuitous lectures, by the professors attached to it, among whom such names have appeared as Birkbeck, Ure, and Combe. The High School behind it was rebuilt in 1821. The Normal School, a handsome Tudor building, is near Garnet Hill, which commands a fine prospect. The Mechanics' Institution is in Hanover Street, near the Andersonian University. The Royal Infirmary, the Blind, and the Deaf and Dumb Asylums, are near the Cathedral, and the Town's Hospital and Magdalen Asylum are not far from these; the former, shaped like a St George's cross, with a dome in the centre. Hutcheson's Hospital or Asylum, with a spire, is in Ingram Street, near the Post Office; the new Lunatic Asylum, at the west end of the town, is in the Norman style.

The most bustling parts are in Buchanan Street, Argyle Street, the Broomielaw, &c.; and in the oldest quarters are Trongate, High Street, Stockwell Street, &c., round the cross; in Bridgegate stands the steeple of the old Merchant's Hall; Woodside and Elmbank are two of the finest crescents, not far from the Kelvin. The West End Park is said to be one of the finest in Britain. At Port Dundas, the Forth and Clyde canal terminates; and at Bowling,

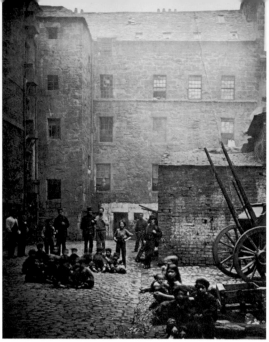

Above, left and right: The contrast between Cathedral and backstreet slum is noteworthy. From the 1870s attempts were made to demolish the slum housing in the city and a fabulous record by Glasgow photographer Thomas Annan was taken of the shocking housing conditions mentioned opposite.

Below: In contrast, one could sail from Glasgow to the most beautiful countryside in the world – the Western Highlands and Islands, via the ships of David MacBrayne.

some miles down the Clyde canal terminates; and at Bowling, some miles down the Clyde, near Dumbarton, is a Pillar to the memory of Henry Bell, who tried the first steamer on the Clyde, the 'Comet,' in the year 1812. Though the first cotton factory was Monteith's, in 1795, yet calicoes were woven here in 1742, and the check union kerchiefs of linen as early as 1700, at Flakefield.

Glasgow to Iona

There is not within the limits of the United Kingdom a succession of more beautiful or varied scenery than in the route from Glasgow to Oban, Oban to Staffa and Iona, round the island of Mull. Glasgow is an admirable station for the tourist. It is within an easy distance, either by rail or steam-boat, of some of the most celebrated portions of the Western Highlands, and any traveller for pleasure, who finds himself within its smoky and dingy precincts, without having fully decided on the route he intends to take in search of the picturesque, beautiful, and romantic, has only to choose the first conveyance westward, whether it be a Greenock train, or a Clyde steam-boat, or Dumbarton coach, to find what he seeks, and to be gratified. Glasgow itself is supposed to offer few attractions to the tourist, but this is a mistake. Old Glasgow, with all its dirt and discomfort, the swarming wretchedness and filth of the celebrated 'Salt Market,' the 'Goose Dubs,' the 'Gallowgate,' and the 'Cowcaddens' is well worthy of a visit, if it were only to see how quaint, and even picturesque, in misery, are the haunts of the poor population of one of the richest cities in the world; consequently the traveller should not omit to take a glance at these places and the Wynds, which will be sufficient. Glasgow is in other respects an interesting place. Forty years ago, there were scores of towns within the limits of the kingdom which were superior to it in wealth, extent, and population. It has now no superior or equal except London. It has a larger population than Edinburgh, Dublin, Liverpool, or Manchester; and combines within itself the advantages possessed by the two last mentioned. Like Manchester, it is a city of tall chimnies and daily increasing manufactures; and like Liverpool, is a commercial port, trading extensively with every part of the known world. Its population amounts to nearly 330,000 souls, of whom 60,000 are Irish. Its prosperity is entirely owing to the industry, perseverance, and intelligence of its inhabitants. The new city of Glasgow, which is rapidly rising to the north-west of the ancient town, is one of the most splendid in Europe, and is not surpassed for beauty of architecture in its public and private buildings, the length, breadth and elegance of its streets, squares, and crescents, even by Edinburgh itself – renowned in all these respects though the latter may be. The motto upon the city arms is 'Let Glasgow flourish.' It has flourished, and bids fair to flourishing more.

There are several routes from Glasgow to Oban. One is by steam-boat from the Broomielaw, down the magnificent river Clyde as far as Bowling; from Bowling by railway to Balloch, at the foot of Loch Lomond; from Balloch by steam-boat on this renowned lake, up the river Falloch to Inverarnan, at the

Above, left: Glasgow's first railway was the Garnkirk & Glasgow, used to carry coal into the city from the Monklands. It is no coincidence that it terminated close to the Tennant's chemical works, with the tallest chimney in Britain, and access to both Monkland and Forth & Clyde Canals.

Above, right: The harbour at Bowling, on the Forth & Clyde Canal, was used to lay up paddle steamers over winter.

Left: A stunning brochure cover for the *Columba* and *Iona*. *Columba* was the longest Clyde steamer and lasted from 1879 until 1935, when she was scrapped.

other extremity; and from Inverarnan by coach to Inveraray and Oban. The tourist by this route has the advantage of seeing Loch Awe, and its mighty lord paramount, Ben Cruachan, a loch and mountain not so much spoken of as Loch Lomond and Ben Lomond, but by no means inferior, and, in the estimation of many, far superior to them both. Another route to Oban is by steamer to Ardrishaig at the entrance of the Crinan Canal, through the Crinan in the track-boat to Loch Crinan; and from Loch Crinan in another steam-boat to Oban, the whole distance being performed in less than twelve hours. By this route the tourist passes through the pretty Kyles of Bute, and amid the magnificent coast scenery of the mainland of Scotland and the island of Mull. The whole of this district is classic ground, and the reader of modern poetry will be reminded at every turn of the paddle-wheel of some incident recorded in poem, song, or drama, by Ossian, Sir Walter Scott, Wordsworth, Joanna Baillie, Thomas Campbell, and others.

The third route, which requires some pedestrianism, is equally attractive. From Glasgow to Greenock by rail, from Greenock to Kilmun, on the Holy Loch, by steam-boat; and from Kilmun along the side of Lock Eck to Strachur, a walk of 18 miles brings the traveller to the shores of Loch Fyne, where, if he does not relish another walk of 10 or 12 miles round the head of the loch, he can take the ferry, and be rowed 5 miles across to Inveraray. From Inveraray to Dalmally, and from Dalmally to Oban, which will afford the pedestrian two days' delight amid some of the most magnificent scenery in Scotland, including the river Achray and its beautiful falls, Kilchurn Castle, Loch Awe, Ben Cruachan, the Pass of Awe – worthy of its name; Connell Ferry, Loch Etive, and Dunolly and Dunstaffnage Castles, renowned in many a song and legend, and deserving all renown, not only from past history, but for the present grandeur of their ruins, and splendour of their sites.

At Oban, during the summer season, a steamer plies regularly round the island of Mull, calling at Staffa and Iona. Mull was pronounced by Dr Maculloch, in his *Hebridean Travels*, a 'detestable island,' but other travellers have not participated in his dislike. On the contrary, Mull is pronounced by all who have sailed round it, or set a foot on it, to be a magnificent island; and though not possessing the advantage of good roads in the interior, and being in other respects in a very primitive state, it possesses manifold attractions for the sportsman, tourist, botanist, geologist, and the man who loves now and then to see human nature as it exists out of the beaten tracks of civilization. But as Iona and Staffa offer attractions of another kind, and enjoy a fame that extends wherever the English tongue is spoken, the great majority of tourists are in too great a hurry to visit them to spend much of their time in Mull. The island, moreover, is not rich in hotel accommodation, except at the one inn of Tobermory, the only town in the island.

Iona, or Icolmkill (the Island of Colm's Church), may be truly called an illustrious spot. It would take a volume to do justice to the claims which Iona has upon the attention of both the scholar and traveller.

Above: The steamer *Linnet* on the Crinan Canal in the 1880s.

Above: Two views from a Caledonian Railway bookmark of about 1905, advertising the Clyde Coast resorts and the new Central Station.